Off the Main Road

JERRY W. MIXON

BROADMAN PRESS
Nashville, Tennessee

4250-15
ISBN: 0-8054-5015-7

Dewey Decimal Classification: B
Subject Headings: MIXON, JERRY W.//CHRISTIAN LIFE
Library of Congress Catalog Card Number: 85-19065
Printed in the United States of America

**Library of Congress Cataloging-in-Publication
Data**

Mixon, Jerry W., 1940-
  Off the main road.

  1. Meditations. 2. Mixon, Jerry W., 1940
I. Title.
BV4832.2.M54   1985   242   85-19065
ISBN 0-8054-5015-7

Pilgrim

I shall plant the seed of this fruit on which I dine
By the side of the road—perhaps someday a tree
Will lift its leafy boughs, and its fruit will shine
Down a bleak autumn evening goldenly.

I shall place these sticks together, and some gray day
One following me may see them and pause to start
A quick bright fire along his lonely way,
And its wind-blown flame may warm his hands
   and his heart.

I shall pencil a pointing finger where a spring
Leaps silverly among the rock-strewn grass;
Others will need its clear cold offering,
And perhaps they might fail to see it as they pass.

At the bend of the road I shall build a wayside shrine,
Stone by stone I shall rear it and leave it there,
It may be that some one whose need is as great as mine
May seek it and find new comfort and strength
   in prayer.

Grace Noll Crowell

Foreword

"Reminiscence"

Reminiscence is the activity which, above all others, brings character into focus. What the mind chooses to remember and relate from a mass of sensations, sights, sounds, and smells is inevitably autobiographical. To no group is reminiscing more important than those who have left the country for the city. For them the reminiscence, whether oral or written, helps to put the new life of schedules, crowds, and software in the perspective of older standards and experiences.

This is what Jerry Mixon, a William Carey alumnus, seeks to do in this volume. He helps us to understand the complexities of contemporary life by returning to an apparently changeless existence, one where the distinctions between life and death, faith and unbelief, fulfillment and despair are as clear as those that separate vital rural commodities, sun and rain. While revealing something of his personality to us, Mixon also uses familiar symbols to communicate to the reader the importance of a Christian commitment that is personal in its nature and rural in the simplicity of its faith. Thus, the seemingly eternal truths of rural living are made to point toward a greater and more lasting truth.

J. RALPH NOONKESTER
President
William Carey College

Introduction

Visitors to our country will never know what life in America is like by reading facts in a book. They will never discover America if they only speed down our interstates. Foreign travelers must leave the interstate and move into the countryside. Here off the main road they will see the freedom of America as presented in daily living.

The Christian life is no different. Truth demands more than a hearing. If we only hear truth and make no application to our lives, we have gained nothing. Many have reduced the Christian life to a period of time in worship, workshops, seminars, and training sessions, but for what purpose? Are we striving to simply learn more truth? If so, then what we learn is still of no value to us. Truth is not only to be heard but also applied. *Off the Main Road* is an attempt to take the reader from the classroom experience of truth into events encountered in the laboratory of life. Printed on the pages that follow is a series of events from childhood days in the rural south to the rolling hills of a north Mississippi pastorate. Each situation is presented in vivid detail so others may relive the experience with me. Through humor and tragedy the reader will see truth explode in a banquet of daily experiences. Applications of truth will rise like a flower stretching to face the morning sun. The final result is *Off the Main Road,* a tapestry of the Christian life, highlighted with classroom truth woven to application in daily events.

JERRY W. MIXON

Contents

Country Road, Take Me Home

JOHN 1:12

"But as many as received him, to
them gave he power to become
the sons of God."

There hangs in my study a beautiful picture of a country dirt road winding through the woods. On either side trees and bushes decorate the scene like slender daffodils. In the distance the road reaches to a crest, giving no indication of what lies beyond. This picture was given to me by the wife of our music director while we served First Baptist, Winona. Jean Abrams said God had touched her life one Sunday morning as I related my road experience with Jesus. The painting was her expression of thanks to me for sharing what God had done in my life.

My home community, Lakeview, was located about seven miles out of Hattiesburg, Mississippi. Our home was just up from the old Mixon cemetery. After crossing the railroad tracks, you could make beautiful footprints in our dirt yard. We never had any grass, but we learned how to sweep dirt with a straw broom. Our life was rather common. Dad worked for Dunn's Grocery Store just on the edge of town. Mom stayed home and cared for her five children. Lakeview Baptist Church was only about three miles down the road. My two older brothers, Robert and Joe, my two sisters, Sue and Patricia, and I all loved to walk to church on Sunday night. I remember we would pretend the rocks on the road were diamonds as they sparkled in the light of passing cars.

I'm a little confused sometimes when I go to a revival and they have you stand up on the day of the week you were saved. It is not that I do not believe I am saved. It is that I do not know what day it was. So what I have done, at different times, is stand up on every day of the week. That way, you see, I must have gotten it right in one of those revivals. You see, one summer day, I was walking along this road that ran between the two large lakes in our community. I remember wearing what we called short-legged pants. Of course, I was singing. Country boys do not walk unless they sing.

The songs that came to my mind were invitation hymns that we sang in church. I can still remember singing, "Have thine own way, Lord! Have thine own way! Thou art the potter, I am the clay!" How well do I remember the hot tears streaming down my cheeks for a reason I could not explain. Looking toward the sky with blurred vision I knew something was wrong with my life. I do not even remember how old I was. Yet this event stands out in my mind more than any other experience with the Lord.

Walking along that country road I cried and sang, "Just as I am, without one plea,/But that thy blood was shed for me,/And that thou bidd'st me come to thee,/O Lamb of God, I come! I come!" My dear friend, I tell you, years of tears, of struggle, of pressure; years of grief, questions, doubts, and searching cannot equal that moment in my life. That day a little country boy opened his heart and Jesus came in to stay. That's why you see the country road picture in my office.

I hope you have this experience in your life. Is there a time and place when Jesus came into your life? No pilgrim is ready for this journey without Jesus.

Poor Folks Called Us Poor

MATTHEW 16:26

"For what is a man profited, if he
shall gain the whole world, and
lose his own soul?"

Will Rogers once said, "God must have loved poor people—he made so many of them." We used to tell the story
that we were so poor that even the poor folks called us
poor. We never had hot dogs; we had "got dogs." There
were seven of us in all. Mom would put the wieners in the
middle of the table and if you got one you were lucky. One
time we did not have any meat, so Mom painted her finger
red, slipped it between the bun and handed it to me.
When I asked, "Where is the wiener?" she whipped me
for losing the wiener. One reason I have such a big mouth
is that we could not afford pacifiers, so Mom used door-
knobs.

I was nine years old before I had a pair of shoes. I was
so excited that I walked three miles backwards just to see
my footprints. I walked into the creek, got my shoes wet,
and ruined them. I'm sure you know by now that I am
joking.

The truth is—we were poor. That is to say we did not
have much money. Robert, my older brother, said that
one Christmas Dad ran outside and fired the shotgun up
in the air. He came back in, sat down, and said, "Boys,

Santa just committed suicide." While most of these stories stretch the truth, the fact remains we were poor.

Even though we had a lot going against us we had more going for us. We learned early in life that happiness did not depend on things. We had just as much fun with our homemade play cars as others did with their store-bought toys.

Jesus taught this lesson when He said, "What is a man profited, if he shall gain the whole world, and lose his own soul?" The truth for us to digest here is that happiness is not brought to pass by things. Happiness is an inward peace. This kind of happiness is Paul writing in a Roman jail, knowing that he was soon to die. This kind of joy caused him to write to his friends and say, "Rejoice, and again I say, rejoice."

Our walk in this life will never be paved with joy until we have learned the lesson that happiness is an inward reality independent of outward circumstances.

Beware of Beggar-Lice

SONG OF SOLOMON 2:15

"Take us the foxes, the little foxes, that spoil the vines."

When I was a lad, Robert, Joe, my two older brothers, Sue and Pat, my two sisters, and I all spent many wonderful hours in the woods of the old Lakeview community. I can well remember coming in from an afternoon of playing down by the old creek. Just before we entered the house we always spent some time pulling off the brown clinging matter from our jeans. This beggar-lice, as we called it, served no good purpose. As we rambled through the woods, somehow it always managed to cling to our jeans.

Down through the years we often pick up beggar-lice in our lives. We have things in our character that have become a habit. These habits serve no worthwhile purpose in our lives. Maybe we saw someone else doing it, so we picked it up. Perhaps it is a word that we heard someone else speak and we added it to our pattern of speech. Sometimes it is nothing more than an attitude.

Did you know that most of us can handle with ease the major events in our lives? It is not some great storm in our life that does us in. We are educated to handle these major events. No, for most of us, it is the small things that happen in our lives that cause us to stumble. Not one small thing, mind you. It is all of the little things that add up. Before we know it, we are in trouble over our head. We have allowed "the foxes, the little foxes" to spoil the vines.

Let each pilgrim guard his mouth well, for the mouth is a revelation of the heart. Our eyes need to be protected from seeing some things. There is the camera that places images on our brain that will never be forgotten. Our feet need to be careful where they take us for they are making a trail that others will soon follow.

Listen and hear, for I tell you, we must be careful to watch for the beggar-lice. This would be a good time to have a spiritual checkup and see if we have some of these beggars who are along for the ride. They bring no good into our lives. They will, if we allow them, bring only ruin.

Scooping Up Mayhaws

MATTHEW 14:19-20

"And he commanded the multitude to sit down and . . . he blessed, and brake, and gave. They did all eat . . . and they took up the fragments."

Living in the country you learn to find an easy way to do everything. As a lad I learned you should wait until after a rain to pick up mayhaws. These little red berries make wonderful jelly. However, you can break your back picking them from the ground or off the tree. Instead I waited until it rained a hard rain. The water stood in the area around the mayhaw trees, and berries floated to the top. It was easy to scoop them up by the handful. I could scoop instead of picking.

Life is like that. We should learn to scoop up the blessings of God instead of picking. Most of us want to select certain blessings each day for God to bestow upon us. We usually think of a certain thing that we desire and seek a way we can convince God that it is best for us. Instead, we should look around us every moment and consider all the blessings God has already given us. Most of us have good health. Most of us have a roof over our head and food on our table—usually more food than we need. Those of us who have jobs should thank God we have the opportunity to work. Others may want to give God praise for living in a country where they can seek a job freely. We have the beauty of the flowers and the trees as well as the sunshine and the rain. Many of you may not have good health, but you can praise God for a society that permits you to select a doctor of your choice for treatment.

Do you remember a story in the Bible where Jesus fed the multitude? After taking the five loaves and two fishes, He blessed them and gave to the people. When they had all eaten and were contented, He told them to "gather up the fragments that remained." When they had completed gathering, they had twelve baskets full. My dear pilgrim, do not neglect on your journey to take time to gather up the fragments. Fragments of blessings that God has already bestowed upon you. Take time to do as the old song says:

> When upon life's billows you are tempest tossed,
> When you are discouraged, thinking all is lost,
> Count your many blessings, name them one by one,
> And it will surprise you what the Lord hath done.

Those days in the mayhaw pond have long since come and gone. Scooping berries will no longer be a part of my daily routine, but the lesson I learned of scooping instead of picking is still operative today. You must decide how you will respond to life. Let yourself be given to scooping in the blessings you already have, and God will give you a basketful to share with others.

Don't Play with Snakes

1 PETER 5:8-9

"Your adversary the devil . . . walketh about, seeking whom he may devour: Whom resist stedfast in the faith."

My dad used to tell some of the funniest stories. I remember one day he said, "Jerry, I was driving the old truck down to the creek when I ran over a snake. The snake struck the truck and killed it. Immediately I jumped out and hit the snake with a hoe, but the snake bit the hoe handle. That handle swelled up as big as a log, so I took it downtown and had it sawed up into 2 x 6's. I went on to another store and bought some chickens. Then I went home and built a chicken house out of the 2 x 6's. When the sun went down, all of the swelling went out of the lumber and it choked all my chickens to death. Now, remember, Son. Don't play with snakes."

The Bible gives us almost the same warning when it says, "Be sober, be vigilant; because your adversary the devil, as a roaring lion, walketh about, seeking whom he may devour" (v. 8). There is no place in the life of a Christian for the devil. He is walking on territory that no longer belongs to him. You belong to Christ. Your life is to be yielded to Jesus and Jesus alone. The child of God is to be alert—be watchful—because the devil is always seeking ways to trip you.

Then Dad would say something like this: "So, if you see

a snake, just call me." Oh, what a wonderful lesson for everyone. This is what we should do as Christians everytime we discover the devil trying to trip us. We need not try to outsmart him. We need not hit him with the hoe handle. We should call our Heavenly Father. Peter writes in the very next verse that we should resist. He makes sure that we understand how to resist: "Whom resist stedfast in the faith." Satan is a spiritual force and must be fought on spiritual grounds. You and I must call upon the only power able to defeat him, the name of Jesus. This is how to resist the devil.

Saturday Night with Granddad

REVELATION 3:21

"To him that overcometh will I grant to sit with me in my throne, even as I also overcame, and am set down with my Father in his throne."

Saturday was a special day at our house. It was the day we went to town. Going to town was a real treat. This usually meant we got ice cream. To modern-day folks this may not mean much, but in 1947 we did not have much ice cream.

Our house was in the country. We had running water, but you had to run outside to get it. We cooked inside and went to the bathroom on the outside. Now, we cook on the outside (patio) and go to the bathroom on the inside. My, how times have changed!

Anyway, Saturday was always a good day. If we had worked hard enough to earn money during the week, we could go to the movie and see "Rocket Man" or "Lash Larue." However, Saturday reached a peak in the evening. On Saturday night my mother's father always came to spend the night. Needless to say, Granddad was the "chief storyteller."

There was one particular story that he told every Saturday night. He told a lot of different stories, but he would always end up with this one. Granddad would lean back and say, "Old John was paid to spend the night in a haunted house. Now, John knew this house was not

haunted. You don't believe in ghosts, do you, children?"
We would all shake our heads.

Then he would continue. "One night John heard this
voice out in the field saying, "I'm in the field." John would
yell back, "I'm in the kitchen." Then the voice came back,
"I'm in the yard," and John shouted back, "I'm in the
kitchen." Once again the voice grew louder, "I'm on the
porch." John knew something was getting closer, but still
he called out in return, "I'm in the kitchen."

Granddad leaned forward in his chair. "I'm at the front
door." Then he would relax in his chair, gain all his
strength, and suddenly leap forward crying, "I got you!"
I tell you, it made no difference how many times we heard
the story; we always jumped at the end.

Life is like that. We know the end of the story. We know
that God is going to make everything come out all right,
but sometimes it is a hit and a miss between the beginning and the end for most of us. You know, we loved to
have Granddad around, even though we did not understand all his ways. We did not approve of all that he did,
but we sure loved him. His very presence was enough to
soothe all our childhood woes; and with the magic of
storytelling, he would send us off to bed with our hearts
beating fast.

We may not understand all of God's ways. We may not
approve of all that He allows to happen, but the sure joy
of His presence is enough to calm our fears and send us
off to bed knowing all is well. God is still on His throne.
All is well.

Sunday Afternoon and a Kite

ISAIAH 40:11

"He shall feed his flock like a shepherd: he shall gather the lambs with his arm, and carry them in his bosom, and shall gently lead."

Sunday afternoons at our house were not much different from anyone else's in our little community. During the winter we sat around the fireplace or made syrup candy. Syrup candy was nothing more than thick syrup poured in a plate and sprinkled with pecans. We then placed it in the back room where there was no heat. After several hours, it was cold enough to cut and eat.

Summertime was a different story. Many times we made trips to the river and spent many happy hours in the warm waters of Bouie River. On a good windy day, we would fly kites in the large sagebrush field between our house and Uncle Carl's.

I remember one Sunday we were all in the field flying our kites. These were not store-bought kites. These were homemade. My dad was an expert at making kites. One of his favorites was the box kite. It looked just like a box. He always made it out of a few straight sticks and newspapers.

This particular Sunday the wind was high and the kite went out of my sight. Looking into the sun, I asked, "How do you know the kite is still up there?" Dad did not say a word. He handed me the string. Holding tight I did not see the kite, but every few seconds I could feel the tug of the kite against the wind.

People often ask me, "How do you know God is leading you to do something?" Part of my reply is that I feel the tug. You see, God has hold of my heartstring. I find that everytime I sin there is a little tug. Everytime I feel lonely, afraid, or alone, there it is, that little tug. His Spirit remains in touch with me. I may not see Him. Sometimes the sky is lowering and black; it seems as though my way is lost; then there is this little tug.

God has hold of my life and I feel His gentle tug in my heart. God never pushes me. He does not drag or force me to act. It really is hard to explain, but as Uncle Carl used to say, "It's as plain as the nose on your face."

I know that you as a pilgrim may sometimes feel that you too are alone. Your heart may be hurting. Your vision may be blurred; but have faith, because your Father has hold of your heartstring. You, too, will feel a tug in your heart. That is God's way of gently leading you in the path of righteousness. Follow Him!

Trading Away My Soft Drink

GENESIS 25:31-32

"And Jacob said, Sell me this day
thy birthright. . . Esau said, . . .
what profit shall this birthright do
me?"

It was a hot summer afternoon. The family had all gone to town. I do not remember why but my older brother, Robert, and I had stayed home. The heat was so unbearable we had made a pallet and were lying in the front room just below the window. The cool breeze stirred the air, giving relief to our perspiring bodies. How I came by a large bottled soft drink I do not know. However, I do remember lying on the floor, head propped up on an old brown pillow. My legs were raised and crossed.

Robert, sitting beside me, watched as I allowed the cool liquid to trickle out of the bottle into my mouth. It was like a well in the desert. Out of the corner of my eye I could see Robert licking his lips and trying to find a way to get his hands on my soft drink.

I might have teased him a little like Jacob teased Esau. You remember Esau came in from hunting and was cold and tired. Jacob cooked his favorite red pottage. I can see Jacob standing over the pot, lifting the spoon to his lips and sipping with a smile. Then tipping the spoon, allowing the hot red pottage to drip back into the pot. Esau could stand it no longer.

Neither could Robert. "Tell you what I'll do, Jerry. I

will trade you Booger for that bottle." I could not believe my ears. My brother was going to trade me the best white dog in the whole United States of America. Booger was a first-rate pet. He could fetch a stick, roll over, and even bark like he was calling your name. "Robert," I said, "you must be kidding."

Then I noticed about half of the soft drink was gone. I leaned over to hand him the bottle and we sealed the agreement with a handshake.

Esau did almost the same thing. Jacob said, "Sell me this day thy birthright." Esau felt he was at the point of death and agreed to trade. In one quick moment, he traded his right as the firstborn son for a bowl of red soup.

Beware as you find your way in this world. You will be given many opportunities to trade. Some have traded a few moments of pleasure for a lifetime of bad memories. Some have traded a moment of glory for a lifetime of fear. Many bargained for wealth and in return had given their own soul.

Robert was never able to reconcile the fact that in an hour of intense heat he traded away one of his most prized possessions. Pilgrim, you will want to make sure that what you get is equal to what you trade.

Dodging Dirt Clods

LUKE 9:62

"And Jesus said unto him, No man, having put his hand to the plough, and looking back, is fit for the kingdom of God."

Our house was located next to the Mississippi Power and Light Company substation. Homer Huggins lived across from us and the Malones lived to our right. Between our house and the Malones, there was this large field where they grazed their cows. Just back of this field near our log road to the river was the field they used for growing a garden.

I loved to hide near the fence and while Tommy Joe or Claude plowed with their mule, I'd throw dirt clods at them. All I had to do was pick the ones that were dried enough by the sun to be hard but moist enough to hold together. Things went pretty good for me until they finally discovered the direction of the clods. That's when I jumped on my stick horse and beat it for the safety of my own backyard.

The Malones never could plow a straight row when they had to keep looking back over their shoulder to see where the dirt clods were coming from.

Think about that in relation to what Jesus said, "No man, having put his hand to the plough, and looking back, is fit for the kingdom of God." I think we must remember that Jesus is speaking about the reign of God.

28

Then again the plow they used in this time period was nothing more than a single-handled stick attached to an ox by means of a rope. It was very difficult to hold the stick straight even if you held it with both hands. Now, think how crooked the row would be if you were always looking back and trying to plow straight. The word translated *fit* is a word that means ready for use. Let each pilgrim come to understand that you and I must do what the man behind the plow was supposed to do. In short, he was to give the plow his undivided attention. He could not plow and look back. Lot's wife looked back and turned into a pillar of salt. Don't look back.

This is an important truth. Let us remember that we cannot give our mind to the devil and expect our body to serve God. Paul says, "Let this mind be in you, which was also in Christ Jesus." Again he says, "Whatsoever things are true . . . honest . . . just . . . pure . . . lovely . . . good . . . think on these things" (Phil. 4:8).

Tommy Joe was unable to plow straight because he was too busy trying to dodge my dirt-clod bullets. He could not give his attention to the plow. We, as pilgrims, must not allow our minds to be distracted. We must give God our attention if God is to reign in our life.

A Man in My Room

MATTHEW 5:14

"Ye are the light of the world."

Mother had sent us off to bed. It was cold in the back room where I slept. Through the back window I could see Dad's shirt hanging on the clothesline. It danced like a ghost in the breeze. The whistle of the wind in the cracks around the window made it difficult for a young lad to get to sleep.

After tossing and turning for what seemed like an hour, I finally buried myself beneath the three blankets and drifted off to a light sleep. Some kind of noise awakened me during the night. As I peeked out from under the cover, I saw this dark figure standing at the foot of my bed. Hardly able to move, my lips formed words, but no sound came Finally it came out like the yell of a wild Indian.

"Mother," I yelled, "someone is in my room." I heard a noise down the hall. Like a flash, Mother appeared in the doorway. Fumbling for the light switch, she said, "What in the world is the matter with you?" As the light came on, I could see the "man" in my room was the silhouette of my overalls hanging on the bedpost. The white bare wall behind them gave an appearance of a man.

30

How many times in our life do we allow things to give us fear when there is really nothing to fear at all? I think, though, the greater truth here is that light shows things up for what they really are. Many times in our younger days while on hunting trips or camping out, we would often see an outline of an animal. After careful investigation in the light, we found it was only a bush or a tree.

I believe this is something that pilgrims should do. Jesus said, "Ye are the light of the world." Part of our task is to show things up for what they really are. You, as a child of God, should dispel darkness and reveal things for what they are. The alcohol-related accidents in this century have totaled nearly 1,700,000 deaths on America's highways. Recent figures flashed on my television screen said every thirty-two seconds someone is injured in an alcohol-related accident. Advertisements would have us believe that alcohol is the finest product available.

The duty of a child of God is to show the finished product. Of course, alcohol is only one area. My dear pilgrim, let us in every situation see that, as the light of the world, we remove falsehood and bring truth to light. After all, we are "the light of the world."

Syrup Bucket Lunch

DEUTERONOMY 5:21

"Neither shalt thou desire thy
neighbor's wife, neither shalt
thou covet thy neighbour's
house."

Grammar school days at Rawls Springs were very
happy days for me. I loved the long ride on the school bus.
And during recess we were allowed to play in the edge of
the woods. I remember well how Mom would, with special
care, pack our lunch. She would take a syrup bucket and,
with an ice pick, punch holes in the top. Inside she would
place a couple of biscuits and sometimes even a slice of
bacon fat. On real good days, we had an apple to eat
during recess.

Somewhere along the way, I picked up a story about a
young lad who always wanted to trade his lunch. There
was one schoolmate who never would let anyone see what
he was eating. Our trader knew his classmate must have
something he did not want to share. One day he watched
as the lad placed his bucket beside all the others. During
recess the trader made sure he switched lunches with the
guy who always hid to eat his lunch. When the dinner bell
rang, the trader was first out the door. He picked up the
heavy lunch bucket and made his way around back of the
big tree in the far corner of the school yard. Taking his
pocketknife, he popped the top on the bucket. There star-

ing him in the face were two hickory nuts and a claw hammer.

How many times in life have we longed for something that someone else had? When once we have taken theirs, we find what we had was much better. The devil is like that. Let us remember that the Bible says he is a liar. He never gives us what he promises. Billy Graham once said, "He tells us of the thrill, but never the kill. He tells us of the fascination, but never the association. He tells us of the kick, but never the kickback." God help us as pilgrims to remember we are not to covet what any man has. Being content with what we have is a very valuable lesson to learn in our journey.

A High School Class Ring

JOHN 3:16

"For God so loved the world, that
he gave."

During my high school days, things were financially
pretty rough at our house. Mother and Dad had divorced.
Robert and Joe had joined the Air Force. Sue had married
and moved to Texas. Mother still had my younger sister,
Patricia, and me to put through school. I was attending
school in Petal, Mississippi, because we had moved to
town. On the day we were to receive our high school class
ring, I made my way outside the building to avoid the
embarrassment of not being able to pay for the ring.
Standing beside a trash can that someone had built a fire
in, I felt a hand on my shoulder.

"Mick," Coach Mac said, "all the teachers got together
and they want to give you something." Boy, I was ready
to run. I knew it was going to be about a hundred licks
with the board of education. Then he opened his hand.
There was the most beautiful ring I think I have ever
seen. The day the rings were for sale I had ordered one,
hoping that by some miracle I would be able to pay for it.
This was to be that miracle. "Here," he said, and then
reaching in his pocket he pulled out a piece of paper,
"This is the list of names of the teachers who bought the
ring." With that, he walked away.

34

There was one thing I knew. Without a doubt, one teacher's name would not be on that list. Why, she hated me. She called me by my last name and always gave the most homework. Yes, there was Mrs. Hinton, Coach Mac and his wife. My eyes continued down the list. Then like a rock it hit me. Glaring me straight in the face was the cold hard fact, the name, Miss Cameron. Why did she go and do that? Looking beside each name I could see that each teacher gave a dollar. That is all, but Miss Cameron —she had given two. I learned an important lesson that day. The one I thought hated me the most was the one who gave the most.

In my spiritual pilgrimage I have often felt God was against me. Just like I felt Miss Cameron was. When God placed me in difficult circumstances and demanded that I give my best, he was attempting to make me a better person. Now, when I face those difficult times, I know there is an unseen hand guarding, guiding me safely through this troubled sea. You, too, must remember:

> God moves in a mysterious way
> His wonders to perform;
> He plants His footsteps in the sea,
> And rides upon the storm.

A Lad Called MAN

ISAIAH 35:8

"The way of holiness . . . the wayfaring men, though fools, shall
not err therein."

While a student in William Carey College, I was called as the associate pastor of Petal Harvey Baptist Church. They in turn sent me to their mission church to work with Rev. P. E. Downey. Those years with Brother Downey and his family are some of the greatest moments of my life. It goes almost without saying that most of what I know about soul-winning I learned from this man of God. Rev. Downey was an expert when it came to dealing with people. The people he worked with were the lower income folks who lived along the river and the old river avenue side of town. I remember one individual that we visited one day along with the pastor of Petal Harvey, Rev. O. E. Thompson. When Brother O. E. asked the mother if we could see her son, she refused. "Why, he ain't got sense enough to come in out of the rain. NO, you can't see him." Then she turned, walked away, talking to herself.

Several weeks later, Downey and I returned to the house. He was able to keep the mother in one room while I went into the kitchen to speak with "Man." Man was his community name, not his given name.

After explaining the way of salvation, I asked Man to

pick up the salt shaker. When he did this, I asked him to pick up the pepper shaker. I knew that Man understood what I was doing. I knew that he had enough knowledge and sense to receive Jesus into his heart.

Then I asked, "Man, would you like for me to pray with you and invite Jesus into your life?" He nodded his head yes. I asked him to kneel down by the chair. The next few moments are some of the most precious in all of my memories. In that small dim kitchen Man prayed after me, "Lord, I know I am a sinner . . . I ask you to forgive me for my sin . . . I ask Jesus to come into my heart." Then there was a pause. My ears will never hear a more beautiful sound this side of heaven. Man burst out in his own words, "LORD, SAVE ME."

Several years later I stood by Man's grave. He was not expected to live as long as he did, because of his affliction, but God had been gracious.

Years have come and gone since then. There have been many souls won to the Lord, because I learned a great lesson that day. It is not up to us to decide if men have the intelligence to refuse or accept the gospel. It is our duty to present them with the gospel. The way is so simple that "wayfaring men, though fools, shall not err therein."

Truth Made Simple

JOHN 20:25

"We have seen the Lord. But
... except I shall see in his hands
the print of the nails ... I will not
believe."

Sermons have a way of coming and going. However, I heard one of the greatest sermons that I think I will ever hear. Dr. J. Ralph Noonkester, president of William Carey College, Hattiesburg, Mississippi, was speaking to the student body. We were in assembly the last time before Easter break. I cannot remember his address word for word, but I do remember this. He said, "When you return from your Easter break, I hope you will not say the Lord is risen, but that you will be able to say, 'I have seen the Lord.'"

Here is such an important truth. No biblical truth designed for me will become active in my life until I make it personal. Dr. Noonkester was saying the historical record of the resurrection means nothing to us unless it becomes a personal experience. Only when we can declare "I have seen the Lord" does salvation become a reality.

Through the years I have tried to keep this truth at the center of my personal life as well as my preaching. What good is the truth "my God shall supply all your need according to his riches in glory" if I do not make it personal? How can I feel the security of being "delivered

. . . from the power of darkness, and . . . translated
. . . into the kingdom of his dear Son"? You see, dear
pilgrim, Bible truth, if it is to become personal, must be
claimed. This is to say, I must believe this verse is for me.
After knowing it is for me, then I must act upon the verse.
Find biblical truth, claim that truth, and act upon that
truth. When I have done this, I have made what used to
be a truth a TRUST. I have accepted and acted on what
God says.

This one statement has helped to open up much more
of the Bible to me. Dr. Noonkester may not be a large man
in stature, but in a few brief words, he stood taller than
most men. One thing is for sure: he helped me to stand
taller.

Kwitchyerbellyakin

PHILIPPIANS 4:4

"Rejoice in the Lord alway."

4:11

"I have learned, in whatsoever state I am, therewith to be content."

While serving as pastor of Goss Baptist Church, I saw the need for a recreation program that would help us reach our community. We were far enough out of town that our youth did not have much opportunity to participate in city recreation. During my stay there, we built a beautiful Family Life Center, a community swimming pool, and a church softball field. The church voted one Sunday, while I was away, to name the field after me. Mixon Field is, of course, a source of pride for me. With the help of church members, we built bathroom facilities at the field. On one side we placed in large print this sign, KWITCHYERBELLYAKIN. If you sound this out, it means quit your bellyaching—or stop griping.

While I was in Winona as pastor of First Baptist Church, my son, Jeffrey, wanted to learn to play golf. We started playing and before I knew it, he was beating me. We both made a rule that when we made a bad shot we would not throw our clubs or yell in anger. We decided we would just say, "Praise the Lord." If you could have heard us during those days, you would have thought it was a pentecostal revival out on the golf course. All you could hear was, "Praise the Lord, thank you, Lord, and thank you, Lord, again." I mean every other shot was bad, so we usually spent our time singing His praise.

Do you like to be around people who always gripe? I heard about one man who griped so much that they said he would probably gripe if you hung him with a new rope. Folks, we must learn that attitude goes a long way toward our success as Christians. This is why Paul was such a success as a pilgrim. This is why he could say at the end of the line, "I have fought a good fight . . . I have finished my course." You see, Paul had learned a long time ago that getting mad at the world does no good. He knew that which happened unto him had "fallen out rather unto the furtherance of the gospel." We need to remember to KWITCHYERBELLYAKIN and do what Paul did, "Rejoice in the Lord alway."

Attitude, to a large measure, will determine our altitude as a child of God.

Rounding Third and Headed Home

JOHN 15:13

"Greater love hath no man than
this, that a man lay down his life
for his friends."

The game was close. There were only two runs difference between Goss Baptist Church and Calvary Baptist
Church. We were the home team, but we needed at least
one more score to assure us of the victory. Most teams
would score one or two runs in the last inning, but we felt
like three would be too much to overcome. At least three
runs against our defense was tough to get.

Tony was on second base and Dudley was at bat. We
already had two outs. Dudley took a low outside pitch and
hit it to deep center field. Tony made a dash for third. As
he made his turn, I could tell he was on his way home. The
insurance run was to be a reality. The left center fielder
had placed the ball in the shortstop's hand with a beautiful throw. My eyes shifted to the catcher. He was very
young. Actually Calvary had been short of players and
brought him off the bench. I knew a collision between
Tony and him would be a disaster for him.

My teammates yelled as Bud waved Tony on. Calvary's
shortstop made an excellent waist-high throw home. The
catcher caught the ball and turned to brace himself
against Tony's blow. At that moment Tony pulled up
short of home plate. The catcher reached up and tagged

Tony out as the two faced each other. The catcher smiled, threw the ball back to the pitcher, and Tony walked to the dugout.

We went on to win the ball game with the two runs, but we won something else that night that was far more important. We won greater respect for one of our players who had rather be out than injure someone else. I asked Tony later, "Why did you stop?" He said, "Man, I just could not run over that little fellow."

We live in a society that says, "If I don't watch out for myself, who will?" One evangelist used to say that our American friends have the attitude, "Get what you can, can what you get, sit on the can, THEN spit in everybody else's can." This is a dog-eat-dog type of world. It is refreshing to see pilgrims who would rather suffer hurt and defeat than to inflict it on someone else. Come to think of it, that was a rule of Jesus: "Greater love hath no man than this, that a man lay down his life for his friends."

Thanks, Tony. Your attitude in sports demonstrates a great principle for the Christian life—others.

Who Is to Blame

MATTHEW 6:21

"Where your treasure is, there
will your heart be also."

As the young pastor concluded his sermon on Adam
and Eve, an elderly lady met him down front. She said,
"I would just like to know where do you men think you
would be if it were not for us women? Why, don't you
know that behind every great man there is a great woman?" The amazed pastor was about to answer her when
an old deacon spoke up, "I'll tell you where we would be
if it had not been for you women. We would still be in the
Garden of Eden."

Over the years I have come across people who want to
spend their life blaming someone else for all their woes.
It is true that Eve sinned first, but it is equally true that
when God came back to the garden he called Adam to give
an account. God help us who have been given the responsibility of a home to do our very best in leading the home
toward God.

I well remember one youth in Pensacola, Florida.
Every time he got into trouble it was always someone else
who was to blame. When will we learn that WE must bear
the responsibility for our own lives? Yes, it is true that
parents have great influence. It is true that our school,
peers, society, and the general environment in which we

live play an important role in shaping us. Still, we must come to grips with the truth expressed by Goethe, a German philosopher. He said, "We are shaped and fashioned by what we love." Jesus said it this way, "Where your treasure is, there will your heart be also." The fact remains that we become what we love. Take time today to check your love list.

If you really want to know why you are the way you are, stop blaming others. Sit down and list all the things you love. You may say, "Well, how in the world can I list all I love?" Take first things first. Start with your checkbook. Make a detailed list of how you spend money not used for maintaining your family. Money is a good tool to measure what we love. Next, I would suggest that you write down how you spend your leisuretime. Time and money are two things we put into that which we love.

How much of your time and money has God had today? It's time to stop blaming others and look within ourselves.

You determine who and what you love; and that which you love makes you what you are.

Faith for the Journey

LUKE 17:6

"The Lord said, If ye had faith, as
a grain of a mustard seed . . ."

Does life seem to you like a dead-end street? Do you feel like the fellow who swallowed a doorknob? He just did not know which way to turn. As a fellow traveler, you need to reexamine your faith from time to time. Many today have lost faith in God. Others have lost faith in others. Millions have lost faith in themselves. Faith is a much-needed force to help us maintain our stability in life. Many are asking the question, "How much faith is needed?"

On one occasion the disciples asked Jesus something like this. They were confused because Jesus had put them to a hard task. He had instructed them to forgive their trespassing brother as many times as he turned to ask them to forgive. In distress they cried, "Increase our faith." They were saying they did not have enough faith to live that kind of life. Jesus returned this answer, "If ye had faith as a grain of a mustard seed, ye might say unto this sycamine tree, Be thou plucked up by the root, and be thou planted in the sea; and it should obey you." Was Jesus saying the disciples did not need more faith?

Yes, He was saying that an increase in faith was not needed. He was stressing not quantity, but quality. They did not need an extra measure of faith. They needed to *exercise* the faith they already had. If they had faith the size of a mustard seed, it was small. Small it might have been, but Jesus said it was still enough faith to move a mountain. We seem to reverse it today and say, "If you have faith the size of a mountain, you can move a mustard seed."

When will we learn that to have faith, we must simply have faith? If we are to learn to trust, we are just to trust. In other words, an increase in faith, if it is needed, will come only as we demonstrate our faith. You can read about faith, study about faith, and pray for faith, but it will not be a reality until you act in faith. Take God at His word and act.

In our journey, let us not lose faith in God. Never lose faith in others and certainly hang on to faith in yourself. Let the winds of opposition blow. Stand in the storms of heartache. Fight during the times of disaster. You may bend, but faith will not let us break. Take that small amount of faith you have and do not be afraid to tackle any problem. Jesus has already declared that you have enough faith to move mountains. Just do not move your mountain into your neighbor's path.

Knowing Your Weakness

ROMANS 8:26

"Likewise the Spirit also helpeth
our infirmities: for we know not
what we should pray, . . . but the
Spirit itself maketh intercession
for us."

Do you know your biggest weakness? Perhaps you have
always thought it to be some particular habit. Women
often think their biggest weakness is overeating. Men
usually list lust. All of us have weaknesses, but each of us
share the biggest weakness. It is the most gigantic, enor-
mous, tremendous weakness we face. We do not know
how to pray as we should.

The Book of Romans tells us that "the Spirit also
helpeth our infirmities." Did you know that *infirmities* is
better translated as weakness? The writer then states
that weakness, "For we know not what we should pray for
as we ought." This means our major weakness is that we
do not know how to pray for ourselves. I do not have the
ability to pray in my best interest. Yes, we pray and we
think we have our best interest at heart, but we are limited by human knowledge. Here is the beauty of this passage. God enters in the prayer closet with us. He is there.
He is a part of our prayer. It is wonderful to have a friend
pray for you, but it means much more when that friend
prays with you.

Notice what Paul says: "The Spirit helpeth our weakness." Where we are limited, He is unlimited. Where we

are weak, He is strong. Here is God involved in our prayer life. We can see this sometimes in our prayers as we begin praying one way, then suddenly our prayer changes. Maybe sometimes over a period of weeks, but the change comes.

There is something more to God being involved in our prayers. The last part of verse 26 says, "The Spirit itself maketh intercession for us with groanings which cannot be uttered." This surely means that God's Spirit can utter them, but not man. Why? Because of man's limitation. Certainly they are uttered, but only by the Spirit. If they were not uttered, they would not be a groan but a meditation. The Spirit is speaking sounds. This is God working through the supernatural in our prayer life.

One night I overheard my father and mother talking. It did not take me long to discover they were talking about me. They discussed what was in my best interest. I'll tell you, I went to sleep that night with a lot more confidence in my parents.

Remember, as you continue your journey, that your biggest weakness is not some habit. It is your lack of knowing the best way to pray. However, you may have great confidence because your Heavenly Father is praying with you. Why not stop and pray now?

Watch for the Rainbow

HEBREWS 6:18

"It was impossible for God to lie."

When God gave the world a rainbow, he added much beauty to our already colorful world. To me the rainbow has stood over the years to mean that God will never break a promise. Noah had lived through the Flood under the guidance of God's hand. Afterward God said, "I will establish my covenant with you; neither shall all flesh be cut off any more by the waters of a flood; neither shall there any more be a flood to destroy the earth. . . . This is the token of the covenant. . . . I do set my bow in the cloud" (Gen. 9:11-13). Everytime you see a rainbow, don't just think of the promise of no more flooding of the earth, but think instead that all of the promises of God are sure.

Traveling down this road of life we need some things that are unchangeable. God's Word is that way. The writer of Hebrews says, "It was impossible for God to lie." Then he goes on to say that we who have fled to Him for refuge have a strong consolation. My dear fellow traveler, let not this world with all of its fast, overnight, get-rich plans rob you of the inheritance you have in Jesus Christ. The Bible is filled with many promises that you and I may claim together. Start today marking every promise you find in the Bible.

We do need to remember that promises are in two main areas. First, there are the *unconditional promises* that come to one and all such as: (1) The rain falls on the just and unjust (Matt. 5:45), (2) Whatsoever we sow, that shall we reap, (Gal. 6:7). These promises do not have any conditions. We do not have to do anything to achieve these promises; they are just so. There is a second group of promises that we should call *conditional*. This means that we must first act and then God will act. They are such as: (1) Whosoever shall call upon the name of the Lord shall be saved (Acts 2:21), (2) If we confess our sins, he is faithful and just to forgive (1 John 1:9). As you make your way through life, be sure to claim all of the promises of God. Take time to gaze at the rainbow and remember He has said, "I will never leave you."

True and False

2 PETER 1:16

"For we have not followed cunningly devised fables."

There was a period of five years in my life when God led
me into the area of full-time evangelism. I spent most of
my time in revival work in Mississippi and Florida. One
day while resting between revivals, I had the care of our
two children, Jeffrey and Lanay. It was very near Easter,
and I wanted the family to enjoy some of the tradition of
Easter. However, I wanted our children to know the difference between the Easter bunny story and the Easter
story in the Bible.

Several times during the day I would sit on the floor
and tell the two stories to our children. Special emphasis
was placed on the Bible as a true event and the Easter
bunny story as fiction.

That night the family climbed into the car for a ride.
My wife had been at work all day. The time was right now
to show her just how much I had taught the children that
day. "Jeffrey," I said, "lean up here and tell your mother
what you learned today." I noticed he looked a little puz-
zled. "Son, what I want you to tell her is the difference in
the Easter bunny and the story I told you from the Bible."
His little eyes rolled from side to side. I could tell his mind
was searching for the right answer. Then I prodded a

little more, "Just tell her the real meaning of Easter." He smiled and said, "That's the day the Easter bunny rose from the dead."

My dear Christian friend, you, too, may have a hard time knowing the difference between truth and falsehood. In our time many groups claim they worship Jesus. We must be on constant guard to see that all of our money, time, and talent is channeled into organizations that will honor Jesus Christ. Remember what Peter said, "We have not followed cunningly devised fables." The Christian faith is a true-life event. There really was a man named Jesus. He lived and died. He was raised from the dead and we are His followers. As you travel over this road of life, make sure your time and effort, as well as your money, are used for His Kingdom.

One Battle with Fear

ROMANS 8:28

"We know that all things work together for good to them that love God."

While I was in a revival meeting in Texas, Rick and I had gone to play tennis one morning. Since the family had gone with me as a vacation, Jeff, our five-year-old, went to the courts with us. As we played on one court, Jeff was hitting the ball on the next court. He tried to hit it high, run around to the other side, and hit it again. Between the two courts was a half-inch steel rod that held tension on the two nets. Jeff ran into the rod, which knocked him unconscious. Rick and I did not see Jeff fall, but we heard him hit the concrete. Running over to him I lifted his head to see blood gush out of his mouth. We took him to a water fountain trying to rinse out his mouth. Finally Rick drove us to the hospital. Jeff came out of it with a mild concussion and thirty-two stitches in his tongue.

I can well remember how calm I was during the time we had to act. Once we were in the hospital and Jeff was in the care of the doctors, I sat down in a wheelchair. The nurse said I had blood all over my shirt and was as white as a ghost. It was then that fear began to take hold of me. All of a sudden I began to think, What if the shirt I placed in his mouth had caused him to strangle on the blood?

What if the car had not started? What would I have done if I had been alone? Why did I not watch Jeff better? Questions came as fast as I could think. Fear had moved in when I was no longer active.

This is not to say that we should all be busy all the time. I am not talking about nervous energy. I am saying that we find ourselves in situations where we can no longer do something positive. It is then, as we find ourselves helpless, that fear gains a grip on our life. As long as most of us are able to act in a given situation we feel capable. Then, when we have done all we can, we still feel an obligation. That obligation usually takes the form of fear and worry.

Did you know most of our fears are of the unknown? In general we do not fear that which we can handle. Fear strikes because we do not know what is coming next. Would Jeff be alright? Would there be brain damage?

Then Vicki appeared in the emergency room holding our daughter, Lanay. She almost fainted when she saw the blood on my shirt. At first she thought I was hurt. A few minutes later the doctor explained the situation and that they would keep Jeff for a few days to observe him.

Later that night after the revival service, I sat with Jeff in his room. I remember how I had laid my hand upon his head when he was a newborn and said, "Father, thank you for a son. I'll do my best to teach him to love and honor You. Keep him safe." That's when my fear left. Once I had time to reflect on my Father's goodness and remember that "all things work together for good," I was able to close my eyes and face the night unafraid.

How to Remove the Stinger

MATTHEW 5:44

"Love your enemies, bless them
that curse you, do good to them
that hate you."

While Nathan Harden was serving as pastor of Bluff Springs Baptist Church near Magnolia, Mississippi, the following incident happened to him and his wife Carolyn. It seems that their son, Eddie, had been into everything he could get into that day. Carolyn's patience had worn thin. She told him that if he did one more out-of-the-way thing she was going to put the belt on him. Sure enough, it was not long before Eddie forgot the warning. When Carolyn reached for him, he dashed out of the house. The house sat on brick pillars, so Eddie crawled under it as far as he could. Seeing that he was not going to come out, she said, "You just wait until your daddy gets home. He will tend to you."

Sure enough, when Nathan came in from work, Carolyn related the events of the day. Nathan, tired and already a little angry, made his way under the house. Eddie had moved all the way to the middle of the house near the chimney. When Nathan reached out to catch Eddie by the hand, Eddie said, "What's the matter, Daddy? Is Mama after you, too!" Needless to say, Eddie took the fire right out of his dad's bones.

Learning how to respond to people is very important.

Many times in life you will be called upon to answer a comment such as, "Your attitude is not very good." Perhaps you have had someone say, "I was sick and you did not even come to visit me." Still others will say, "You upset me the other day."

We have to learn to do what Eddie did even though he did not know what he was doing. While I was visiting in one church, a fellow told me right to my face, "You know, I never did like you." I smiled and said, "That's odd. I was rather fond of you." Of course, he had nothing else to say. I took the stinger right out of his attack.

Learning to control our emotions is very important. Jesus said, "Love your enemies, bless them that curse you, do good to them that hate you." I have learned that keeping my emotions at a low level helps me respond with love. One method I have used is to imagine the person who makes the attack in some funny or unusual situation. Immediately, I would picture him wearing a diaper and holding a skunk. Now, it is hard to get mad at a fellow wearing a diaper, much less one holding a skunk. I know this illustration is not very spiritual, but it has helped me avoid head-on collisions with attackers that would have hindered future spiritual relations. Learning to relieve our attackers of their stinger by lowering the emotional level of the conversation will benefit all.

Look to the Hills

PSALM 121:1-2

"I will lift up mine eyes unto the hills, from whence cometh my help. My help cometh from the Lord."

Have you ever stood in the presence of a towering mountain? Somehow you just had the feeling of strength. There stretched high against the backdrop of God's sea-blue sky is this huge piece of handiwork. Standing against the storms of time, it seems to say, "I have stood the test. The winter winds and blistering summers have cut away, but here I stand."

David said, "I will lift up mine eyes unto the hills." David was asking a question more than making a statement. David was saying, "I will lift up mine eyes unto the hills; from whence cometh my help?" He asked where his help will come from. Jewish thought carried with it the idea that God dwelt among the hills. The hills referred to here are the hills of Zion. We, like David, often need assurance. We often ask the same question. Where will my help come from?

Even with these words fresh from his lips, David seems to shout, "My help comes from the Lord!" There is no pagan idea in David's theology. He knows that strength does not come from some earthly mound, no matter how high it reaches toward the sky. His realization is that the God of the mountains will not permit his foot to slip. This trail of life has a constant guard. It is the Yahweh. He, who watches over David, will not doze or nod. David need not be anxious. David faced the same problem we face. He needed help and he knew where help would come from. He just did not know when. The searching question for him was, "How soon?"

Winding down this highway of life, you and I often seek God to act in our behalf and do it now. We are like the fellow who prayed for patience, "Lord, give me patience and give it to me right now." Let the writer of this psalm give us the assurance that help will come to us. That help will come from the Lord. He who created us is near and cares. Jesus said it this way: "The very hairs of your head are all numbered" (Matt. 10:30).

Take time in your journey to look to the hills and remember that your God is in hearing distance and will intervene, but always in His own time. Look, I say, unto the hills.

Walk Through a Cemetery

GENESIS 5:17

"... And he died."

A brief walk through a cemetery can yield a harvest of knowledge. You may find there just how much respect the community has for their dead by the upkeep of the grounds. Words written in marble will give you some idea of the religious convictions of the community. Dates carved in stone will place in your mind the length of time this site has been a part of the community.

Perhaps, even more important, you will come to the realization that death is as much of a part of life as the air we breathe. Do you remember reading in the Scriptures this phrase, "And he died"? This should help us realize that sin does have serious consequences.

The Bible declares the payoff or the wages of sin to be death. There is a serious lesson to learn about sin. We must never take sin lightly. Sin must not become a matter to be ignored or passed over without consideration of the results. Then again we should understand that sin is a process. There was not just one man who died. Over and over the Bible says, "And he died."

This was a chain reaction that had its start in the Garden of Eden. True, Adam and Eve sinned first, but each of us has sinned. There has always been this idea with us that sin is an act. It is an act, but it is more. Have you ever heard someone say, "The way I live is hurting no one but me, so why should it bother you?" This simply is not true. There is no way for sin to be viewed as a single act separated from any other act. Neither can we see sins we commit as unrelated to the lives of others.

If the walk in a cemetery tells us anything, it should remind us that decisions on how we live and act have a great influence on the lives of other people. As you gaze upon the headstones, remember that sin does have serious consequences and that sin is a process. This process never ends until it brings death. The Book of James said it this way: "Sin, when it is finished, bringeth forth death."

Let us remind ourselves during this brief walk that our acts, words, and deeds never go unnoticed by someone. There will always be another person looking to us as an example. Take time during this trip among the dead to ask God to place within you the right spirit to live so that others might find God—knowing well that one day it will be said of you, "And he died."

Be Sure to Make Friends

PROVERBS 17:17

"A friend loveth at all times."

There is a little book on my shelf that has some thoughts from unknown writers. Here are a couple that mean a lot to me. "A friend is the half of my life." "An ounce of loyalty is worth a pound of cleverness." However, my favorite in this section is "He who has a thousand friends has not one to spare." There is a place in our heart that no wife or parent or anyone else can take the place of. That is, a friend.

The Bible says, "There is a friend that sticketh closer than a brother" (Prov. 18:4). If you should sit down today and count on your fingers how many friends you have, most of us could count them on one hand. I do not mean acquaintances. A friend is someone who knows you like the back of their hand. They know your good points and your bad. Even more important, they never give up on you. They always stay in close contact. They are always there when you need a hand. Friends bring out the best in you. Even if your family should fail, a friend will be there. Now, count again and see how many friends you really have.

The Bible gives us a beautiful story of friendship. Saul was jealous of David's success and was trying to kill him.

King Saul's son, Jonathan, was David's friend. Jonathan helped David escape from the evil hand of his father. As they parted, Jonathan said, "The Lord be between me and thee, and between thee and me for ever." Friends do not come and go with the wind. Friends remain with us for a lifetime.

Sometime ago while playing a game of tennis, a friend of mine noticed a young lad playing alone on another court. My friend and the two fellows with him asked this young man to come play doubles with them. His answer was no. One of the guys walked over and said, "Hey, no use for you to play alone, come on over and play with us." At this point the young man stopped, turned around and said, "Are you crazy? I said NO! Now, leave me alone." Here is a young man who has a problem.

If you go back and read Proverbs 18:24 again, you will find that it says, "A man that hath friends must shew himself friendly." Today as you continue your walk through this life, let me ask you to consider not only how many friends you have, but how friendly you have been. You know it does not take much effort to extend a handshake to a visitor in a worship service, but it makes a world of difference to the visitor. Most of the time he will base his impression of your church, not on the pastor, but on the friendliness of the people.

Perhaps as you think now of all your friends you might want to take a little more care in developing friendship. You might want to take time to show others that you are a friend. You might want to spend less time talking and more time listening. Some of the greatest moments of my life have been time just spent with friends. I can well remember that some of the most difficult times leaving a church field have been saying good-bye to special friends.

There have been many times in my life when I have simply sat alone and wept because I missed my friends.

Your journey will take you down many roads and you shall have many opportunities to be a friend. Take time to have friends and to be a friend. You shall do well to remember your greatest friend. "What a friend we have in Jesus,/All our sins and grief to bear!"

Be Not Deceived

GALATIANS 6:7

"Be not deceived."

The crowd began to gather around the store window. "Look, they are fighting," cried one lady. The sign in the store window read, TRANSPARENT CHINESE DRAGON FIGHTING FISH! The owner had placed a bowl in the window filled with water only. As the people grew in number, so did the cries. "Look, can't you see the ripples on the water?" "They must be fighting," cried another man. The people were so gullible that one lady ordered a pair to give as a gift. After the owner told them of the hoax, the crowd walked away mumbling to each other.

Down through the years, men have fallen for a wide variety of different hoaxes. One tale is that a mythical emperor paraded down the street in his birthday suit. He had been convinced by a pair of rogues that he was wearing splendid new clothes.

Perhaps you have heard of Ferdinand Waldo DeMar. He is better known as the Great Imposter. He has posed as a schoolteacher, a monk, a zoologist, a prison warden, and a college professor. In 1951 he was deported from the Royal Canadian Navy because of his impersonation of a surgeon. In 1970 he appeared as the pastor of a small thirty-five-member conservative Baptist church located in the Washington Island hamlet of Friday Harbor. The Reverend DeMar says he accepted Christ as his personal Savior in 1958 and brought to an end the life of an imposter.

The Christian church has often been faced with those who attempt to fool us. Jesus chose twelve and one of them was an imposter. The church today has many members who are imposters.

The early church had a creed and it was not Jesus as Savior. It was Jesus is Lord. This is the type of attitude we need today. Let each of us take off our mask. Let us display the real person. God help us to realize that until we know what kind of persons we are, not even God can help us. As a child of God, remember God has made an investment in you that no company, no cooperative, and no organization in the world will make. He has invested His only Son.

You are not a carbon copy. You may die trying to be like someone else, but God did not intend for you to live that way. He wants you to allow Him to live His life in you. That way you will not deceive yourself and will not be deceived by others.

The word is, "Be not deceived."

Don't Walk with Worry

ISAIAH 26:3

"Thou wilt keep him in perfect peace."

Someone has suggested that "died of worry" should be written on many grave markers. Many end life because of worry. This problem of worry is a major concern today. Dr. Edward Podolsky has stated that worry can be the root cause of such physical disorders as heart trouble, high blood pressure, forms of asthma, rheumatism, ulcers, colds, thyroid malfunction, arthritis, migraine headaches, blindness, and stomach disorders.

What is the cause of worry? Most of us would agree that it is usually fear. We fear the unknown. We do not know what is going to happen next, but we still have to deal with the future. One way to deal with it is by worry. One lady said, "Preacher, don't tell me that worrying does not help . . . why, almost everything I worry about never happens." The father worries whether he can maintain his job. The farmer worries over his crops. Parents worry over children. Children worry about acceptance by their peers. The businessman worries about the rise and fall of sales. The young worry about pimples, while the old worry about wrinkles. We all have our worries, but we do not have to.

The Greek word for "to divide" is *merizo*. The Greek

word for "mind" is *nous*. When you combine these two words, you have the Greek word *merimnao,* which means worry. Thus worry is a division of one's mind. Worry divides our thoughts. The Bible declares, "A double-minded man is unstable in all his ways" (Jas. 1:8). Worry affects our thought process. Worry affects our physical life. Worry affects our spiritual growth. There is no part of our life that worry does not affect in a minus. Worry is never a plus. Worry is never positive; it is negative. Since worry affects our mind, it in turn will cause us to make judgments that are invalid. We cannot think straight when we are worried.

The next time you are afraid of the future and begin to worry, combat worry with faith. There is no better way than to pray. Isaiah said, "Thou wilt keep him in perfect peace, whose mind is stayed on thee: because he trusteth in thee" (26:3).

Worry is doubt, but prayer is faith. It is up to us to decide how we will face life daily. Will we face it with worry and doubt, or will we face it with faith and prayer?

Confession of a Traveler

1 JOHN 1:9

"If we confess our sins, he is faithful and just to forgive us our sins."

What should a Christian do when he sins? This is a question that has bothered many a traveler. Some would have us believe that if we sin, then we were never saved. Others would have us believe that if we sin and die before we confess, we will still not be saved. If any passage of Scripture shoots this kind of thinking down, then 1 John 1:9 should be fired at the enemy. "If we confess our sins, he is faithful and just to forgive us our sins, and to cleanse us from all unrighteousness," according to John. Notice that God does not forsake us when we sin. We will not always be faithful, but He is. We may feel that He has forsaken us, but He will not. Hebrews 13:5 says, "I will never leave thee nor forsake thee."

We are told here that when we sin we should confess. Notice the writer does not say if we sin. He knows that we are going to sin. He says, "If we confess" when we do sin, then we will be forgiven. Now, confession is more than just telling God we have sinned. It is more than being sorry for our sins; it is admitting them with the full intention and desire to forsake them. It is true that we may not be able to forsake them on our own, but the willingness is present. When we have confessed our sins, we can rest assured that God will continue to be just. *Just* means that God will always do what is right. We don't, but God does.

What, then, is just? Well, first of all, to be just means God does what is right. To do what is right means He will keep His word. His word is that if we confess, He forgives. To be just means that God will continue to be faithful and just. Psalm 103:12 says, "As far as the east is from the west, so far hath he removed our transgressions from us."

Now, how far is that? Why, it is the "farthest extremity"; or we may say that God will go to any length to separate our sins from us once we have confessed them to Him. That's why Hebrews 8:12 claims, "Their sins and their iniquities will I remember no more." Man forgets by mistake, but God forgets by choice.

Once a boy who was afflicted in body and mind gathered weeds for flowers. He wanted to carry them to his mother who was in the hospital. His brother had beautiful roses. The father tried to discourage the afflicted boy from taking the weeds into her room, but failed. Seeing her two children, one with flowers and one with weeds, the mother thanked John for the roses and then wrapped Jimmy and his weeds with equal love and care in her arms.

God is like that. We bring to him what we are—not what we hope to be, but just what we are. God is able to forgive and make us to become better persons.

My son thinks Dad can fix anything. In his younger days, he would bring item after item. His words were always the same: "Fix it, Daddy, fix it." This is how we need to come to our Father every time we sin. Fix it, Father, fix it; and He will.

Hit the Jackpot

1 PETER 4:16

"If any man suffer as a Christian,
let him not be ashamed."

The story is told of two preachers who visited Las Vegas. While on their visit they decided to take a firsthand view of the city. When they entered one of the casinos, they separated so they could cover the building quickly. Of course, you know they were giving out tracts to those who would accept them. One minister made his way to the card table, while the other went in the direction of the slot machines. These one-armed bandits react as you act. All you have to do is drop in a quarter and bingo, you will hit the jackpot. You will be a winner.

Well, that's what they want you to think. Many of us go through life with this kind of attitude. We somehow feel that we are going to make the big discovery that will solve all our problems and answer all of our questions, not realizing that each day has its own problems and its own answers. Only crackpots look for jackpots. Well, can you believe this young preacher became interested in the slot machine. He thought to himself, *What's a quarter? Do you think I might hit the jackpot? Just think how much good I could do with all that money.* Then quick as a flash, he dropped in his quarter and turned to look around to see who was watching. Then it happened. Why, he never thought of this. Perhaps the most embarrassing thing happened: he lost his quarter.

Most of us would have liked a happy ending to the story. You wanted the guy to win. We want to win the jackpot. We often think that at the end of the rainbow there just really might be a pot of gold. How sad it is when the Christian faith has been passed off as the jackpot of life. Get saved and all of your problems are over. Truth is, get saved and most of your problems will start.

Salvation does not protect us from all the problems of life. Nothing could be further from the truth. There is no jackpot. God promised a life of discipline. He does not call just believers, but behavers. He does not seek just a decision, but disciples. Perhaps if we examine the word *Christian* in the New Testament we can better understand. Actually the word *Christian* appears only three times in the Bible. The first appearance is in the Book of Acts. Here it is a name given to the followers of Jesus. A revival had broken out after the death of Stephen. Laymen had preached the gospel. The results had been amazing. The church in Jerusalem heard about the revival. They sent Barnabas to find out if it was true. Barnabas, in turn, brought Saul, who had been converted; and there they preached for a year. The unbelievers became so convinced of the life-style of these followers that they began to call them Christians—meaning people who were like Christ. The Bible says, "The disciples were first called Christians in Antioch" (Acts 11:26).

The second appearance is in the same book. Paul was brought before King Agrippa. He made a plea for the king to become a follower of Jesus. The king replied, "Almost thou persuadest me to be a Christian" (26:28). The third and final use of this word is 1 Peter 4:16, "If any suffer as a Christian, let him not be ashamed." Just from these places we can see that being a Christian has nothing to do with finding a rainbow pot of gold or hitting the jackpot.

The Christian life is no easy road, but it is the best road. The Christian will have to suffer in this life. It is a part of the struggle of men as well as saints. Remember, let no one sell you short on the Christian faith. Be prepared for the journey, and remember, "The God of all grace, who hath called us unto his eternal glory by Christ Jesus, after that ye have suffered a while, make you perfect, stablish, strengthen, settle you" (1 Pet. 5:10).

Miracles Along the Way

JOHN 11:1-44

"He cried with a loud voice, Lazarus, come forth."

Have you ever come home to find the usual evening greeting cut a little short? The house is cleaner than usual. No matter what you say, there seems to be a cold shoulder from the mate. Suddenly, it hits you like a bolt of lightning. Today is her birthday and you forgot. Quickly, without a word, you leave. Down at the local store you purchase a box of candy. Then returning home you enter without knocking only to be greeted by the wife who says, "Oh, honey, my birthday, and you remembered. It is a miracle."

What a common usage of a great word. If a team who is the underdog puts a better team to defeat, we say it was a miracle. If Junior passes the exam, we declare this to be a real down-to-earth miracle. If our friend has an operation and is able to walk again soon, we say, "This is a walking miracle." Aside from this common use of the word, let me remind us that in our journey we do see God at work in the miracle area.

Jesus performed his first miracle at the wedding in Cana of Galilee. Even prior to his performing the miracle, men were asked to fill the pots with water. Again in John 11:1-44 we read of the raising of a man named Lazarus from the dead. He had been dead for several days. Notice that before Jesus raised Lazarus He asked that the stone be rolled away from the door. Here is man's part. Man should always be willing to do what he knows how to do. We must be willing to do the possible. The impossible must be left up to God. Let us remember in our journey that there are many situations when we ask God to act and do a miracle, but we are not willing to first do the possible. God will do the miracle, but we all have a part.

Can you think of a gap that exists between you and a friend? You have been asking God to bridge that gap, but to no avail. The miracle just has not happened. Think now—what have you not done that would help bridge the gap? Have you shown your concern for this person? Have you shown yourself friendly? Have you in any way set forth love to this person? Have you done the possible and set in motion the law that allows God to do the impossible?

Remember, there are some stones that we can roll away before God will raise the dead.

A Word About Prejudice

1 JOHN 2:10

"He that loveth his brother
abideth in the light."

We had taken a group of our youth and adults to the Sunshine School in Marianna, Florida. Our purpose was to work with those students selected by the school staff in Vacation Bible School. These students were mentally retarded. The staff had selected about thirty clients, as they were called, for us to teach that week. I remember our first session. Several of the clients came in with football helmets on. Of course, most of us began to laugh and say things like, "Hey, what position do you play?" We were not being ugly, just sort of joking around. We did, though, render a judgment. We thought they were wearing the helmets just because they wanted to or to get attention. We were told later by the staff that these were special students who were prone to fall. The helmets were to protect them. Needless to say, we said nothing else about their wearing the helmets.

Prejudice is like that. When we see someone and we render a judgment of like or dislike, most of the time we do it without bothering to get the facts. How many times have you heard someone say, "I don't like her"? When you ask why, he says, "Oh, she reminds me of someone else I don't like." The child of God must have no place in his life for hatred. Whether a person is black or white makes no difference to God. You, as a pilgrim, will have to deal with many different people in life. You must learn to treat each person as an individual. Take time to gather information and get all the facts before you render a judgment.

We used to sing a little song in our Bible School at Lakeview.

> Jesus loves the little children,
> All the children of the world,
> Red and yellow, black and white,
> They are precious in His sight,
> Jesus loves the little children of the world.

The poet Thoreau once said, "It is never too late to give up our prejudices."

This Record Will Stand

MATTHEW 12:36

"Every idle word that men shall speak, they shall give account thereof."

Dr. Wayne Dehoney, retired pastor of Walnut Street Baptist Church in Louisville, Kentucky, related this story in one of his sermons. "In 1899 a football team from a small college in the mountains of Tennessee left their home to play five major college teams in six days. They won every game.

"They defeated Texas University 12-0, and the next day played Texas A & M. When the game was over, they had won 32-0. The very next day they beat Tulane 23-0. The following day was Sunday, so they did not play. On Monday they took on L.S.U. and eased by them 34-0. Tuesday they came to Mississippi and battled Mississippi College (Baptist college). They did manage to slip by Mississippi College by a score of 12-0.

"Think of this now. They scored 113 points in five days and nobody scored on them. Before the season was over, they played another seven games and won all seven. Many believe this to be the greatest college football record ever. Congratulations to Sewanee College in Sewanee, Tennessee."

Records are important. In the field of sports no record stands for long. Almost as soon as the records are made, they are broken. There is something to be said here about the Christian experience. You and I are making records. God has some way to record every act and every deed. The Bible says, "Every idle word that men shall speak, they shall give account thereof." Why do teams keep records? They do so because when they come to the end of the season they want a measuring stick to see how well they have done.

We do not want to get into the details of a Great White Throne judgment and the Judgment seat of Christ; but I do want to impress upon you, pilgrim, *all of us* will give an account of ourselves to God. This should cause us to pick our words carefully. The idea of a judgment should help us be diligent in our efforts to reach others with the gospel. The final judgment should give us even greater willingness to open our lives to the leadership of His Holy Spirit. We do need to do as we used to sing: "Oh, be careful little ears what you hear/Oh, be careful little eyes what you see/for the Lord up above is looking down in love/Oh, be careful little hands what you do."

Symbol of Remembrance

LUKE 22:19

"This do in remembrance of me."

Suppose you are about to take a trip away from your home for a while. You may even be gone a very long time. You do not wish to be forgotten, so you try to select an important event in your life and call your family to remember you by this.

Jesus Christ faced this problem. He knew that soon this physical presence on earth would be over. He wanted all of His followers to remember Him. Perhaps He thought of the great sermon He preached on the mountain. It is amazing that many times as you go back to a former church no one comes up to say, "I remember that great sermon you preached." No! Instead they say things like, "I remember you coming over to the house the day Mother died," or "I really want to thank you for visiting with my family during our son's illness." What folks will remember will be the things you did, not the things you said.

Jesus could have chosen many different words, deeds, or events. His birth was unusual enough. Many of His miracles would certainly be worth remembering. Yet, He called them to remember Him in this fashion. When Jesus came and sat with them at the table, He took the bread and blessed it, saying, "This is my body which is given for you." Then holding the cup He said, "This cup is the new testament in my blood, which is shed for you." We must notice the all-important words, "This do in remembrance of me." Jesus chose for us to remember Him in what we generally call the Lord's Supper.

It is important as we travel that we carry memories with us. The most important memory a Christian has in what God did for him is Jesus Christ.

Jesus calls us to remember Him, not in a cradle but on a cross. The symbols of remembrance are:

> not the angels, but the mob
> not the manger, but the mount
> not the child, but the Christ
> not the cradle, but the cross
> not peace, but suffering

The symbols of remembrance are not:

> the Christmas tree
> the gifts
> the lights

BUT they are the broken bread and the warm red wine (or juice). This, Jesus said, "Do in remembrance of me."

Take a Little Salt

MATTHEW 5:13

"Ye are the salt of the earth."

The followers of Jesus must have been a little shocked when He said, "Ye are the salt of the earth." What did He mean? Was He giving an option? Notice He did not say, "If you don't mind, please be the salt." He did not say, "If you have the time, be the salt." He said, "Ye are the salt." There is no choice. Once you have identified with Jesus you are to the world what salt is to people.

Salt was a means by which meat was preserved in New Testament times. Now, we do not need salt to serve us in this manner today, but we do need to preserve some things just as salt did then. We, the Christians, are supposed to be a preserving force for good in our community. We preserve the truths of God. We preserve the home, the church—all the things that are worth preserving. Then salt always adds flavor. A Christian should bring a different flavor to every situation. If people are telling dirty stories and you walk up, the stories should cease—simply because of your presence. If you belong to a club, your presence should add a spiritual flavor to that club.

Have you ever had peas with no salt? They taste terrible. Wherever you put salt, it will have an effect. So we

82

who are the children of God should have an effect in every situation. The effect should always be for good.

If you continue reading, you will find that Jesus said, "If the salt has lost its savour . . . it is thenceforth . . . to be cast out, and to be trodden under foot of men." The salt Jesus spoke of was from the Dead Sea. When used to preserve meat, the leftovers were always picked up and reused. Soon the container would be filled with more impurities than salt. It would no longer do the job. The salt had lost its effectiveness. Sometimes we are like that salt. We become so mixed up with the world that we lose our effectiveness as a child of God. Notice the salt was not thrown on the grass because it would kill the grass. Instead, it was thrown in the path where men walked. I believe Jesus is saying that when you and I become so like the world that we lose our witness, men will simply ignore our words just as they walk over the salt in the path. That's why we need to keep our prayer life up to date. We need a little salt for the journey.

Look Above the Storm

MATTHEW 14:24-33

"O thou of little faith, wherefore
didst thou doubt?"

The cool water tickled as it gushed around his legs.
Every muscle in his body was tense. His eyes were on
Jesus. His thoughts were gripped with the excitement of
the moment. Finally, with shaking hand he released the
side of the boat. He stood upon the waves. Peter was doing
the impossible. He was walking on water.

Jesus had approached the boat as it was being tossed in
the sea. The disciples heard Him say, "Be of good cheer;
it is I, be not afraid." Peter had cried, "Lord, if it be thou,
bid me come unto thee on the water." That is how Peter
came to be in the situation at this point.

Quickly he began to walk. Every eye was on him.
Slowly at first, with trembling feet, he moved away from
the security of the boat. Only a few feet more and he
would be at the side of Jesus. Then something happened.
His eyes shifted. He looked at the trees, noticing they
were bent almost to the ground by the gushing wind. The
cool night air was like fear, cutting his breath till he was
gasping for air. The whitecaps seemed larger and a salty
spray dashed against his side. A startled group of disciples peered over the side of the boat into darkness. The
sound of the wind carried a cry for help to the straining

ears of his fellow disciples. "Lord, save me" rose from the lips of Peter, now sinking beneath the sea. Jesus stretched forth His hand and caught him.

Why did Peter sink? There are two unchanging facts. First of all, Peter's feet did not change. Secondly, the water did not change. How in the world, then, could he be walking on the water one minute and sinking the next? Since neither of these two changed, what did change? Listen again, as the story continues. The Bible says, "When he saw the wind boisterous, he was afraid; and beginning to sink." Peter left the boat, operating on the principle of faith. That is believing what God says is true no matter what our physical senses tell us. Then out in the waves, he took his eyes off Jesus and began to look at the storm. The storm caused him to lose faith. When he lost his faith, he lost his footing. Now, this is an important lesson for all of us who are pilgrims. Life will have many storms. There will be many rough days, but keep your eye on Jesus.

Remember who you are. Remember where you are going. Remember He is the Master of the storm. Remember it is He who has bid you take this walk through life. Do not believe in your own sense. Trust God and His word. Jesus pulled Peter to his side and said, "O thou of little faith, wherefore didst thou doubt?"

Remember, don't look at the situations of life and allow them to cause you to be afraid. Keep looking above the storm—there is a silver lining.

Don't Look Back

PHILIPPIANS 3:13-14

"But this one thing I do, forgetting those things which are behind."

All of us have a weakness to look back. Truth is that
looking back usually does us no good. We all remember
how Lot's wife looked back and was turned into a pillar
of salt.

The Holy Spirit speaking through Paul says, "Forgetting those things which are behind." This is an important
truth. Some time ago I heard of a mother who had three
children playing with four other friends in the backyard.
Things became quiet, so the mother looked out the back
door. The children were sitting in a perfect circle with a
mother skunk allowing her eight little ones to have
breakfast. The mother dashed out the door screaming,
"Run, children, run!" At which time each child picked up
a skunk and ran.

Many of us are like that. We are carrying around something out of our past that is just a bad odor. One of the
ideas we have expressed here is that we need to forget the
past when we have come clean with God and been forgiv-
en. We are told in the Bible that God does not remember
our sins against us anymore. Neither should we. Paul
says something else here, too. He does not want us just to
forget, but he also wants us to reach. Here are his words:

"Reaching forth unto those things which are before." Let us seek the truth that in our journey through this life, there are many things in our past that we need to forget. Now, when I say forget, I do not mean that we have no memory of them. We forget by mistake. God forgets by choice. If I am trying to forget something and I keep telling myself to forget it, I find that everytime I say forget it, I remember it. It is my firm belief that Paul does not really wish that we forget the past. We must learn from the past; and to do this, we must remember.

So what, then, is he saying? Paul is saying, "Forget the past and reach out in the present." This, to me, means that I do not allow the past to hinder the present. You know, when God forgives, he forgets. He remembers the sin against us no more. That is, He does not allow the past to hinder relationships in the present.

I struggled for years trying to forget all the bad things people had done to me. I labored under the knowledge that if I could not forget I had not forgiven. That simply is not true. The way I know if I have forgiven someone is whether or not I allow the past event to influence present relationships. The same is true here. Paul is saying learn from the past; but as sure as forgetting wipes out memory, so you and I must not allow our past sins to hinder us in the present journey.

A Walk Through the Woods

ISAIAH 30:7

"Their strength is to sit still."

Dark brown leaves smushed quietly beneath my feet as I made my way off the main road. The morning air was cool and crisp. Rainfall during the night had sprinkled the forest with a wet beauty amid this winter season. Oak leaves left hanging on the trees seemed poised and waiting to be blown to the ground. Some dried by the morning sun made a cracking sound as they fell against the branches of the trees. There alone in God's forest, cedar and pine trees still stood tall like green giant sentries guarding the forest.

In the distance sounds from the highway mingled with the call of a black crow circling above. Standing alone in this winter paradise I felt the presence of God. No strong ill winds blowing. There was no burning desire to act and no real earthshaking experience. Still I felt a presence. An unseen companion who silently slipped into my mind with the words, "Be still and know that I am God."

How sad, I thought, *that others are not able to experience this with me.* The truth is that most of our high spiritual moments do not come in a crowd. Not even in church, but alone, shut up with God, we are able to respond and sense His presence.

Perhaps we are all too busy. Modern society rarely ever takes time to meditate. Not pray—just meditate. Utter no words, just allow our mind to be open to Him. Not even to gain new spiritual truth. No desire for direction. This is just a meditation to know Him. Most of the pilgrims will not have the luxury of a forest. It may be difficult to find a time and a place to be alone with God. One thing is certain. If we are to ever be more like Him, we are going to have to get to know Him better.

So, pilgrim, make time to be alone with God. You will find this to be a refreshing shower in His love. We need time to pray. We need time to read our Bible, but we also need time to meditate oñ God. We can learn a lesson from the prophet in the Old Testament who said, "They that wait upon the Lord shall renew their strength; . . . they shall run, and not be weary, and they shall walk, and not faint" (Isa. 40:31).

Look at Your Hands

ISAIAH 49:15-16

"Yea, they may forget, yet will I
not forget thee."

During my early ministry I came to the point where I said, "God, I'm tired of trying. I'm tired of working. I'm tired of preaching. It seems that the more I do, the more I see that needs doing. I'm tired of trying to help people who don't want any help. I'm tired of being used. I'm tired of seeing my family hurt. Really, God, I'm just tired of You."

My Bible was open and my face buried in its pages. I was waiting for a bolt of lightning. I had finally spoken words I never thought I would speak. Nothing happened. Then a still small voice within seemed to say, "I know. Anything else you need to tell Me?" Why, it was like a breath of fresh air. It was a cool drink on a hot summer day. It was a warm fireplace on a cold winter night.

Maybe for the first time in my life, I realized that God was not like man. He knows everything. He knew how I felt. Part of my problem was that I needed to tell God how I felt. I needed to allow myself to be honest with God. He had always been honest with me. During this time, I came to realize that God did not love me because I was doing His preaching or visiting His sick. He loved me for *who He was,* not for what I was doing.

90

Then again I had pushed myself so hard that I felt as though God had walked off and left me. He was nowhere to be found. I remember reading in Genesis that the Bible said, "And God remembered Noah." Did this mean God had forgotten Noah? Did all of a sudden up in heaven God say, "Oops, now let me see, where did I put Noah? Oh, yes, he is in the ark. I have got to get him out of there." No! God never forgets us. Isaiah reminds us how important we are to God. Can a mother forget her child? Yes, millions do. Then God goes on to say in Isaiah 49:15-16, "They may forget, yet will I not forget thee." We need to hear this. I needed to hear this. God was telling me He knew how I felt, but I needed to remember He would never leave me or forget me.

Do you know what part of your body you know more about than any other? It is your hands. You see your hands more than you do your face. You look at the palm of your hands more often than you do the back of your hands. Now, listen to what God says: "Behold, I have [written] thee upon the palms of my hands; thy walls are continually before me." Glory! Glory! God has not forgotten me. He has not forgotten you. He knows where we are on the journey and how we feel. When I learned that lesson, the walk with God became a road with one less rough spot.

A Cross in the Sand

1 CORINTHIANS 2:2

"For I determined not to know any thing among you, save Jesus Christ, and him crucified."

As we travel along this road of life, it sometimes does us good to stop along the trail and draw in the sand. I have drawn pictures of various things, but most often I find myself drawing a simple cross. The cross always reminds me of Jesus.

Jesus, God's unspeakable gift. No wonder the writer of John's Gospel cried out, "There are also many other things which Jesus did, the which, if they should be written every one, I suppose that even the world itself could not contain the books that should be written" (21:25). Jesus, the man who suffered. Now, you and I are called to take His yoke upon us—to suffer with Him—to be in light afflictions and to die daily. When we take our hat off to a card-carrying Christian, we must remember we salute one who suffers.

Jesus is a dynamic person, not a vague principle, not some impersonal ideal of philosophy which claims my supreme allegiance. His is *character*, not *concept*. Christmas tells of His arrival and Easter tells of His survival. He is always for us and never against us. He is persistent in providing us with survival benefits.

He meets every need and solves every problem. Jesus

is the bread when I am hungry—the water when I am thirsty—the heat when I am cold—the sun when it is raining. Romans 5:1 says He is the peacemaker. First Corinthians 5:7 hails Him as the sacrificial Lamb. Second Corinthians calls Jesus the Image of God. Paul walks through Galatians crying, "the Liberator" (5:1), and Ephesians 4:13 sets Him as the goal of Character.

Jesus is the sweetest name I know—There is something about that name—Jesus—Jesus—God's final word "the expressed image of HIMSELF"—the one true man—God in the Flesh—Jesus—oh, how sweet the name.

Jesus—Neither length of time nor frequency of experience has dimmed or diminished my conviction that Jesus Christ is all that is stated above. He is that and more! One never defines Christ, only confines Him to a mode of expression that can be understood.

Jesus—the light unto my pathway and the lamp unto my feet. With Him no path too dark, no road too rough, no wind too strong, and no event too big. Jesus, blessed Jesus—the cross in the sand always reminds me of Jesus.

Building Bridges

1 TIMOTHY 2:5

"For there is one God, and one
mediator between God and men,
the man Christ Jesus."

Cold waters rippled across jagged limbs lodged in the middle of the stream. White foam formed, then slowly drifted out of sight. Golden brown leaves seemed to dance momentarily upon the waters as the swirling wind tossed them across the current. Green moss edged its way down the bank as if to drink from the passing stream. High above was the massive concrete structure held together with steel rods. Spread across the banks of this country stream stood this huge token of modern man's ability to build. Because of this bridge children could now be driven to school with ease. Farmers carried produce to market. People came from distant places to visit with old friends who had moved to the country. Often this bridge became a platform for young lads to cast a fishing line. Some would only pause long enough to throw a rock at passing debris. Today it was my hideout for meditation.

How can it be that in a world of division we have found ways to cross every stream, climb every mountain, explore the ocean floor, fly beyond the moon, but we have not yet learned to conquer the human gap of race? We can build bridges over mighty rivers but still find ourselves helpless to span the chasm of hatred for others. How is it that we are successful in scientific matters, but failures in relationships?

We have not as a nation given ourselves to the needs of the poor. Our elderly feel like outcasts while our young think they have been neglected. God help us to see there are many bridges to be built.

Bridges may be built in human relations by kindness. Sometimes a link may begin with a smile or a handshake. Many nations have become allies because of the friendship of her leaders. Many strong bridges exist today across streams that were first crossed by an old log. Let all my fellow travelers meditate with me today about bridges. We must remember the biggest gap that ever existed was between a righteous God and sinful man. The bridge between the two was built by a man—Jesus Christ.

It is time now for each of us to allow our lives to become a bridge that unites.

Words Softly Spoken

PROVERBS 15:23

"A man hath joy by the answer of
his mouth: and a word spoken in
due season, how good it is!"

The preacher wakes to the ringing of the phone. The
voice on the other end says, "Preacher, I want you to
come over here right now and talk to my wife. She is the
coldest woman I know." That may seem a little too distant for many of you, but let me say, it is not as far out
in left field as you may think.

Let us back the story up a little. The alarm went off at
five in the morning. He managed to drag himself to the
shower. At breakfast he hardly said a word. After his
third cup of coffee, he left for work. He was gone all day.
His wife was home with two children. The washing machine broke down and she had to go across town to wash.
Jimmy, the baby boy, spilled her new bottle of perfume
while playing in the bedroom. Johnny, the toddler, cut his
finger on a bottle he broke trying to climb onto the kitch-
en table. All day she has worked, washed, cleaned, and
cooked. About five-thirty he comes home with hardly a
hello. Once in the house he finds the newspaper and reads
it through. During supper he does ask, "How was your
day?" When she spills the beans, he pays little attention.
After several hours of watching television, he slips into
the bedroom. He does not bother to take a bath. Sliding

across the bed he puts his arm around his wife, saying,
"Would you . . . " only to be discouraged as she turns over
to face the wall. He sits up and says, "I'm going to call the
preacher. You are too cold."

Now, look at his actions. He has been Frosty the Snow-
man since five o'clock that morning. He has not taken the
time to show any interest in her at all. She has been
cooped up in the house listenting to the be ba . . . da da
. . . Mama . . . childish geese gabble of two children all day.
She wants some intelligent conversation. One of the first
complaints wives make about their husbands is: "He does
not talk to me anymore." Have you ever wondered why
a guy as ugly as a fence post could marry a beautiful girl?
He knew what to say. You see, women love with their
emotions and their ears. That's why she cried on the day
you were married. Her emotions were involved more
than yours. That's why you better not forget the anniver-
sary—she is emotionally tied to that day much more than
you are. Listen, fellows, a woman not only loves with her
emotions, but also her ears. She needs to be told she is
pretty. She needs to be told the supper was excellent. She
needs to be told the house looks great. She needs to hear
you say, "I love you."

Pilgrims with partners need to live together with har-
mony. Perhaps if you as a husband will do a little more
talking to your wife, you will not only find all your needs
met, but there will be no phone calls late in the night.

Three Bad Shoes in the Church

PSALM 26:2

"Examine me, O Lord, and prove
me; try my reins and my heart."

The sun was beating down as I lifted the shovel out of the large hole the three of us were working in. A local contractor had hired me on one of his crews. After spending the last three years in the Army behind a desk, I was pretty soft. As I sat down on the ground, one of the black men on the crew said, "Preacher, did you know I is a preacher, too?" I smiled and said, "You may be a preacher, but I think you are preaching for the wrong side."

"Naw, man, I mean I used to preach ... but somethin's happen ... and I don't preach anymore. I was a good preacher ... would you like to hear my favorite sermon?" I took my hand and smoothed the dirt so I could rest my back against the cool, fresh-dug earth. Leaning back against the moist ground, I waited for his theological discourse. He climbed to the edge of the hole.

Standing on a mound of dirt, he raised his hand and said, "It is called 'Three Bad Shoes in the Church.' The first shoe looks pretty good. When you walk up to it and speak, it speaks right back. I mean ... it don't say nothing bad. All it says is good ... it has a good sole ... no holes

98

. . . it has a good tongue, but if you look real close you will find it has a 'bad eye.'

"This is the man or woman who loves to read those materials that are not fit to read. This is the young person who loves the movies that appeal only to his natural desires. This is the person who is always looking for the worst in people. He is got a bad eye."

At this time a truck drove by and we all jumped into the hole and started digging. The boss drove slowly by, but did not stop. I kept digging and my friend kept preaching. "Now, the second bad shoe in the church is . . . well, he got a good sole. I mean he knows the Lord. His eye is good. He would never look at that kind of material. He looks for the best in people and he is careful about the movies and television. His problem is not his soul . . . not his eye, but if you look underneath you will see this shoe had a bad 'tongue.' He is critical. He is negative. He never has anything good to say about anyone. His mouth is full of gossip.

"Now, look at the last shoe. Check out his eye . . . good eye . . . take a look at his tongue . . . good tongue. He has a good shine. Turn the shoe over and look at the sole. The sole has a hole in it. Everything is good about this shoe, but his 'sole.' He speaks well of others. He does not go to bad movies . . . and would never read dirty books. His problem is he is too good. Not too good for God, but too good to see his need for God. He will never get to heaven because he is depending on his works . . . and you know the Bible says we are saved by grace and not by works. That's it! 'Three Bad Shoes in the Church.' What do you think?"

What my friend had to say that day did make a lot of sense. We all need to take a look at our soul from time to

time. We need to watch what we view with our eyes and
we certainly need to choose our words with tender care.
Three bad shoes in the church—well, I'll say, he certainly
made his point.

A Portrait of Melissa

ROMANS 8:28

"All things work together."

The death of Melissa Breazeal was a shock to the entire city of Winona. In the final weeks of her senior year, graduation was not to be. Early that Friday morning on a rain slick highway, she lost control of her automobile and crashed into an overflowing stream. Melissa was an outstanding Christian and a member of First Baptist Church of Winona, Mississippi. On the eve of her funeral I was asked to speak in a special memorial service in which only the senior class was present. Here are some of the remarks I made to the class that night.

Welcome to the real world. Here on the edge of your senior year of high school you have been thrust into the reality that life is not to be easy. There are many difficulties and hardships ahead. For years now parents, teachers, pastors, and friends have paved the way for you. They have, to some degree, been a shield for your protection. You have been cared for on every hand, but this you must face yourself. The death of a classmate is shocking. Then again, so is life. Those of you who have a strong faith in God will

find peace and comfort knowing that Melissa
was a Christian. Others of you may become
bogged down attempting to explain or understand her death.

There really is no worthy way for us to explain
what has happened. We must accept death as a
fact of life and continue to live. I hope today you
will not see just this accident but will look at the
whole of her life. The Bible declares the phrase,
"All things work together." This means that
when Melissa's vehicle left the road that morning God was present through *being* and *knowledge.* In that moment God continued to work in
her life. This little phrase, "work together,"
means overseer or one who is managing affairs.
In the hours that followed, God pieced the entire
life of this young lady together to produce one
final image.

Many of you will see only pieces of that portrait. You will isolate one solitary event. Many
of you will remember only her death and forget
the beautiful life she lived. We can, if we allow
ourselves, see only what we have lost and not
what she has given us. This will be a tragedy!
God, on the other hand, looks from her birth-
place to this rain-swollen stream. God is span-
ning eighteen years of a well-lived life. He is
placing all of the pieces together to produce the
final portrait.

I believe the final stroke of that painting was
by Melissa. I have in my hand a notebook. Melissa filled these pages with notes from preachers
she heard speak. In May of this year she visited
with the Methodist congregation in Vaiden. Re-

marks made by the pastor are recorded in this book. The final stroke of the brush was the mark of Melissa's pen. Just days before her death Melissa Breazeal wrote these final words in this book: ... "We shall never die ... spiritually we live eternally as the children of God."

We Would See Jesus

GALATIANS 4:19

"Until Christ be formed in you."

There is a little sign on my pulpit. It carries a very brief message. The message is a motto that I have adopted not only for my preaching but for my life. Dr. J. D. Grey, former pastor of First Baptist Church, New Orleans, Louisiana, gave it to me while preaching a revival in my church. The sign reads, "We would see Jesus."

This matter of allowing Jesus to be seen in our life may be considered in this manner. If we see the person of man as presented in 1 Thessalonians 5:23—your whole spirit and soul and body—perhaps we can understand it better. The body is that which identifies us with the physical world. The spirit is that which identifies us with the spiritual world. The soul may be divided into intellect, emotions, and will. Actually, every decision we make is made in the soul. The soul is the darkroom of the film processing plant. Here in the darkroom is where we process all information received and then decide how we will act. In other words, when God speaks to us, he does this by His Spirit. That Spirit contacts us through our spirit. The Spirit moves upon the intellect of man (Heb. 10:17).

When the intellect hears, our emotions become involved. Emotions will be a factor in our decision-making

104

process. This is one reason so many people are saved
during a worship service. The emotions reach a very high
level during the invitation. The surroundings are spiritual. Everything is being done to sway the emotions toward a decision to receive Christ. Then our will plays the
final role. It is here in the soul that the will decides to
accept or reject Jesus as Lord.

Now, there are five physical senses that we live by in
the physical world. They are taste, touch, sight, smell,
and hearing. I believe we have at least three spiritual
senses by which we live in the spiritual world. First, there
is intuition—knowing something but not knowing how
we know it.

Second, we have the Word of God. The Bible is plain
physical evidence on which to base our life in a physical
world. The Bible is physical evidence presented in a spiritual sense. Thirdly, we have an enlightened conscience.
Man's conscience gives him a sense of right and wrong.
It is never good to follow your conscience because it can
be coached to accept bad if everyone else is accepting it
(1 Tim. 4:2). However, a Christian has a conscience that
has been enlightened by the word of God. For example,
Jesus said, "Whosoever shall smite thee on the right
cheek, turn to him the other also."

Put all of this into what we have just talked about.
Immediately when you are struck you must decide how
to react. Will you now live by the physical rule of life, or
will you live by the spiritual law? The moment you are
struck your emotions will become involved. Your blood
pressure will rise. Most people will be tempted to strike
back immediately. That's why it is important to know the
Bible. God's Word helps us learn how to act and react in
this life. Our enlightened conscience has been told by the

word of God that our best course of action is to turn the other cheek.

Intellectually we know this. Our emotions are running high, and it is at this point that our will springs into action. Our brain relays a message to the muscles in the arm—tighten . . . strike. Quick as a flash, our arm is brought over our head and we strike back. That is spiritual defeat.

This is why Paul said to us, "Let this mind be in you which was also in Christ Jesus" (Phil. 2:5). The mind is the key.

So many times our youth return from retreats only to find they return to the same old lives in a matter of days. After a little investigation, you can usually learn they have not prayed early in the morning. They had no daily devotions, and the company they kept was not helpful to their Christian lives. While on retreat they were in prayer and Bible study daily. They were with friends who helped. Their minds were on spiritual things. There is no way we can read and listen to the trash of this world and at the same time serve Jesus. You cannot give your mind to the devil and your body to God. The power that controls the mind controls the body.

Return now to the situation. You have been struck. Your emotions are running wild. Quickly you remember the words of Jesus. You do not understand how His advice will help or if it will work. Only in faith do you operate. Your mind tells your hand to relax. Your mind says, "Turn the other cheek."

I tell you, in that moment and in that situation, the life of Jesus Christ has been formed in *you.* Jesus is living in your life—someone else has just seen Jesus expressed in your life. Your body did just what your mind told it to do. To be carnally minded (like the world), Paul says, "is death" (Rom. 8:6). If we live on the physical sense of the world, we are defeated. However, he also says, "To be spiritually minded is life and peace." This is another way of saying that if we are minding the Spirit, we will have life and peace—the life of victory because Jesus Christ has formed His life in ours. We would see Jesus.

Angel in My Pocket

MATTHEW 18:10

"Take heed that ye despise not
one of these little ones; for I say
unto you that in heaven their an-
gels do always behold the face of
my Father."

Something seemed to be wrong. I had never been this far from shore before. I struggled against the current, but it was no use. My feet could no longer touch bottom and I began to go under. Gasping for breath I shouted, "Help!" Helen Ashley, the relative who had carried O. C., Jerry Wayne, and me to the river, was already in the water. As I went under for the third time, I remember looking up and seeing daylight through the muddy water. A hand reached out and took hold of my hair. I remember that feeling of helplessness. Unable to breathe, I still managed to assist in the rescue by dog paddling. The next thing I remember was coming to on the bank of the river. Helen was sitting on my back pushing hard to revive me. The first thing I said when I spoke was, "Get off me—you are heavy."

There have been many experiences in my life since then in which I was brought close to death. Somehow in the back of my mind there remains this constant feeling that God has placed his hand on my life for some special reason. My mother tells of an experience early in my childhood when I was unable to keep any food on my stomach. The doctor told her he had done all that he could and it looked as though it was in the hands of God. Mom said that night during her sleep her mother appeared at the foot of her bed. "Hazel, give Jerry . . . " The mixture Mother no longer remembers, but in a matter of hours I was better.

Leaving Hattiesburg one day I came to a junction of Highway 49. The right of way was mine, but as I approached the intersection an inner voice said, "That transport truck is not going to stop." Quickly I jammed the brake, only to see the truck speed through the intersection. My life had been spared again.

Kneeling in the middle of the football stadium, I remembered many happy moments on that field. But now my whole world had crashed in on me. Everything that could be near and dear to a young man seemed to have left. Tears streaming down my cheeks, I lifted my head toward heaven. "God, here is my life. I have made a terrible mess of everything. If you can use me, I am willing to be used." I believe beyond a shadow of a doubt that God used every event in my life to bring me to this point of surrender. Here I would give to Him everything. Now I was in search of that special reason for which I felt I had been protected.

The mind is a terrible thing to waste, but it is even worse to waste a life. I have not yet fulfilled all that God wants me to be and do, but I have given all to Him.

I hope that you as a pilgrim can come to face the truth that God has something special for you. There is a place for each child in His kingdom. You can have the assurance that you are a part of His plan. There is no way for me to express my thanks to God for His protection or His

plan for my life. My goal is to be ever ready for each door
He opens for me to enter.

Take a fresh look back over your life. See the hand of
God as He has led you through troubled times. Find your
place in His Son.

Breaking Up—So Hard to Do

JOHN 14:2

"In my Father's house are many
mansions: if it were not so, I
would have told you. I go to prepare a place for you."

We had spent most of the morning filling each box and
bag we could with items from the house. Each time Mom
would pack something away she would cry. We had spent
several very happy years in this house in Petal, Mississippi. Now, Mom's health was bad and she could no longer
live alone. When the last load pulled away from the
house, I remember standing in the drive and looking back
one last time.

The thought that came to mind was that someday we
will not have to break up homes anymore. In my brief life
I have seen homes broken because husband and wife
could no longer communicate. Homes had crumbled
under the weight of grief because of the death of a son or
daughter. I had witnessed the breakup of homes within
my family as well as my church. There are so many be-
liefs held sacred that the breakup of a home destroys for
the parties involved. Backing out of the drive I turned my
headlights on and faced the dark road ahead. Slowly I
moved onto the main road, giving thanks for the hope of
no more broken homes.

Jesus gave us a beautiful promise when He said, "I go
to prepare a place for you." These words raced through

my mind. Just think, a home that we can never lose. Growing up had been difficult for me because we had moved a number of times. On one occasion we moved twice in one day. I remember one night when Pat and I moved most of our furniture in the back of my car. She drove the car and I held beds and other items in the trunk to keep them from falling out. "No more breaking up home—no more moving"—there is a place prepared for me in heaven. We had never lived in a prepared place. I mean, every house we lived in was prepared for someone else.

Heaven is prepared for me. I have spent long hours thinking about heaven. Not only is it a prepared place, but it is a promised place. This is not a promise made by someone who cannot keep it. Several times we were promised a house, but for some reason or another we never got it. This one in heaven is a promise from God. We would do well also if we remember that it is a place. Heaven is not some ideal. It is not a concept. Heaven is a place.

Most of the time when I come home the family greets me at the door. I do not push them aside and walk over to the sofa and greet it. I do not kiss the table and chairs. All of these comforts help make my home a nice place to live, but that which makes my home a home is my family. That which makes heaven a place and a place worthwhile is Jesus. Thank God there is coming a day when no one will have to break camp again. There will be no more broken homes by death, divorce, or any other reason. God will make all things new. The hope of that eternal home in heaven has served me well. The hurt of seeing homes break up has also helped me to do all that I can to keep my home together in the Lord.

Some time ago I heard an evangelist speak on the

home. At the close of the sermon he said, "Whatever you
are going to do to keep your home together, hurry." Let
me ask you as a pilgrim whatever you are going to do—
whatever you need to do to keep your home together—
hurry, hurry, hurry!

The Popcorn Tree

COLOSSIANS 2:6-7

"Rooted and built up in him."

My father-in-law gave me a popcorn tree. On the coast they grew to be about ten feet in just a few years. When we returned home, I found a pot and planted the tree, being careful not to damage the roots. It was kept safe in the carport of our home. Several days later I noticed it was not doing too well.

One afternoon during this time I was mowing the lawn and receiving the help of my five-year-old son, Jeffrey. We were working at this time in the flower bed. I had cut down several small scrub trees that had taken root. The axe had made a cut in the ground and Jeffrey broke off a limb from one of the scrubs. He placed the limb in the open cut and packed the dirt around it. In his broken English he said, "I grow a tree." "Sure," I said, fully intending to pull the ugly limb up once he went inside.

After our mowing was over, I took the small popcorn tree and began to nurse it. I mean I took every care with that tree. Somewhere I had read that if you talk to plants it will help them grow. If talking is good, then singing may be even better, so I sang to the popcorn tree. A few days later it died.

I have since learned to my great relief that it was not

my singing that killed it, but the fact that it did not have enough soil. A popcorn tree needs to have a source of soil that is unlimited. How true this is of Christians. We often limit God in our lives because we do not believe that He can do anymore than we can do. How big is your God? Do you serve a Christ who can do anything in keeping with His nature and character? Second, I learned that a popcorn tree needs the elements of weather. It needs sunshine and rain. Too much of either or the absence of either will kill it. What a lesson for the child of God. If we are to mature and grow as Christians, we need not only the good times, but we need the bad.

As I walked about the yard looking for broken limbs to pick up, I noticed a small uninvited guest in my flower bed. There standing tall amid the flowers was Jeffrey's scrub tree. I had forgotten to return and pull it up. There alone in this wind, rain, and sunshine his tree had grown several inches. The roots had dug into the unlimited amount of soil, and growth was the result. While my tree—protected, pampered, and petted—had died, Jeffrey's tree, exposed to all the danger of normal living, had stood the test and lived.

As Christians we, too, must stand in the normal avenues of sickness, pain, and suffering. We, too, must learn that it is in the sunshine and rain that we grow. This growth is possible only if we are living in a God who is not limited. This is a good day to take a soil sample of your life.

The Time Is Now

GALATIANS 6:10

"As we have therefore opportunity, let us do good unto all men, especially . . . the household of faith."

When the phone rang in General Kelly's office, one of the other aides answered. I was busy doing some typing. Although I was in the infantry I had been assigned as an enlisted aid to General Kelly's office. When I learned the call was for me, I assumed it was one of my friends. The lady on the line very calmly shared with me the news most of us dread. Hearing of my father's death was a shock. Several days later our family gathered in the cemetery in Hattiesburg, Mississippi. I remember standing beside my Dad's grave and thinking *I'm sorry, Dad. Sorry I never took the time to say I love you. Sorry we did not have more time together. Sorry that you and I were not better friends. Sorry I never told you about my friend, Jesus. Sorry, Dad—I'm sorry.*

Time in this life is short. We are here but a brief period. We shall do well to spend more time with our loved ones. Duty of country and community are important. Duties to family are of the utmost importance. How many of your brothers and sisters have you spent time with lately? How easy it is to pick up the phone and send a brief hello to a family member. I have noticed that most of the people I visit in rest homes have the same complaint. They feel they have been forgotten.

Not too far out in the distance for most of us there will come a day when we shall bid them farewell. Their eyes will close in death, and we will remember all those lost opportunities when we almost wrote them a letter. We will think of all the times we could have visited with them. Our hearts will be heavy, for we will remember all those things we did not do.

While this is true of our earthly family, it is also true of our heavenly family. Think about all those friends in the church who have helped you along the way. Many of them now are old and gray. A word of thanks from you will be like water to a thirsty man. Take time today to write a special note, make a phone call, or visit with a brother in the faith.

When you stand before their graves, you will not have to say I'm sorry.

Supper Time

Some time ago I wandered along the old pathway. It was the path that ran from our house to Uncle Carl's. It seemed as though the grass was always greener along the sides of this well-beaten path.

My brothers, Robert and Joe, and my two sisters, Sue and Pat, and I used to run down this lane playing cowboys. We would hunt wild game, play hide-and-seek, and swing from the trees on vines. Those that were not too green we tried to smoke.

Late in the afternoon, Mother would come to the back of the house. She would stand on the steps and call, "Supper Time." Her voice wound its way down through the trees, vines, and flowers and entered our hut or den or playhouse. No matter what was being done at this time we stopped. Once again ten feet could be heard as they pounded their way down the path. Pushing and shoving our way through the back door, we took our place around the table.

It made no difference to us if we had syrup and bread, bread and gravy, or if it was just soup. The warm feeling in our house did not come from the stove. The joy, the fellowship, the love, and the warm spirit were produced by my mother.

Many were the times she stood for hours over an old washtub in the backyard and scrubbed our clothes. I have seen her prime the old pump when it looked as though the water she poured in was going to freeze.

She put up with our rebellion, our times of fighting, our ugly words, our questions, and our moments of despair. She did not just stand up for us; she stood up with us. No matter what kind of trouble we managed to get ourselves into, she came and stood right with us.

If we were wrong, she punished us. If we were right, she complimented us.

My father was the head of our home, but Mother was the heart. She was there when we needed her. She cut out many a paper doll for Pat. She made many doll dresses for Sue. She helped Robert and Joe build a clubhouse. She showed me how to tie a knot in a string and how to make a cup and saucer with thread.

Mother remembers many things about our childhood, but one thing from mine stands out above all others. She remembers that Pat and I built a play church. Then we would take turns preaching to each other.

I remember many things such as the frogs, the cats, Scotty and Booger, my two favorite dogs. I remember my first taste of green tomatoes in the garden. However, one of the most outstanding things in my mind is still the old path. There we would be building a fort to fight off the enemy. Our plans were made, our guns were ready; and then bouncing from tree to tree came those delightful words, "Supper Time."

I will not see Mother this Mother's Day—I'll not be in the playhouse—nor in the lane. I'll be standing in my pulpit to preach the good news of Jesus Christ which my

mother taught in word and deed. Then one day when this
journey has come to the close, I shall hear those grand
and glorious words, *Supper Time.* I'll close my eyes and
sit down at my Father's table forever and ever.